CLEAR
ENGLISH

—

Frank & Andrew St George

BLOOMSBURY

First published in 1996 by
Bloomsbury Publishing Plc
38 Soho Square
London W1V 5DF

Copyright © 1996 by Frank and Andrew St George

The moral right of the authors has been asserted

A copy of the CIP entry for this book is available
from the British Library

ISBN 0 7475 2613 3

10 9 8 7 6 5 4 3 2

Jacket design by Sarah Maxey
Text design by AB3
Typeset by Hewer Text Composition Services, Edinburgh
Printed in Great Britain by Clays Ltd, St Ives plc

Contents

___

For
Kate St George

Foreword

—

The five sections of this book are important in specific ways, and each will apply to you at different stages of your writing. Read the *Introduction* and *The Principles* for inspiration and suggestions about writing; then while you are writing, refer to *The Principles* at the appropriate stages of planning, thinking, writing, rewriting and ending. If you have a problem with a point of usage, the answer may be in *The Uses*; if the problem will not disappear, try saying what you want to say some other way. We wrote the *Clear Grammar and Punctuation* section so that the way we talk about language is clear, just as a surgeon talks about parts of the body. If you want to know what a noun is, you will find the answer there. The last section, *Clear Essentials*, is a summary of the guidelines included in the book.

However you choose to read *Clear English*, we hope you will use it to check your daily or professional reading and writing for clarity and accuracy. Use our principles to ask of everything you write: Is it clear? Is it accurate? Does it have style? We hope you will carry this book around and refer to it. We hope you will pause to think about our examples and to write a few of your own. And we hope you will read *Clear English* as you should any book: with scepticism, attention and intelligence. Above all, we hope you will find it rewarding. We know it will help you to write better.

1. *Introduction: Clear Style*

All writing is creative. Everything you read has been written: shoe sizes, road signs, novels, newspapers and instruction manuals. Behind every word you see is the writer who wrote it. Words are written everywhere. Is writing easy? It can be. Is it hard? It can be. If you write without thought and effort, you may be read without pleasure or understanding. But if you apply your intelligence, knowledge, experience and personality, you will succeed. These are the best, most effective and portable resources you have.

Almost everyone can write something; but fewer can write well; still fewer write as well as they could. This book is designed to promote better writing in all areas of life and to help readers develop their own clear, strong, distinctive and personal styles. We do not intend this to be a weighty grammar book, nor an exhaustive guide to punctuation, spelling and rhetoric.

The information here condenses the wisdom of many grammar books and dictionaries combined with our experience of writing in business, journalism, education and in specialist fields like biography and social history. We have written this book to help you. We suggest the guidelines and principles because they work. Following your own star in matters of language is, for everyone, a test of nerve: we hope you will aim for perfection.

As well as expressing your individual style, good writing should reflect your need to communicate clearly, to convince, persuade or cajole your readers and to influence their thoughts and ideas. Words can make things happen, convey information, demonstrate knowledge or express feelings. And the way we write is just as much an expression of who we are as how we speak and the way we dress. The more clearly and stylishly we write, the better the image we project of ourselves.

To write well you must **concentrate** and **focus**. Have a clear idea of what your purpose is in writing, and ignore distractions. Ideas change as we go along. New information becomes available. A deadline looms. But you have to start somewhere. Ideas *will* come. Remember four questions:

- What am I saying?
- What do I think about it?
- What will the readers think?
- What am I trying to do?

Start by looking at the **sense** of what you are writing. Be clear about who you are writing for and feel confident that what you have written will be understood. You must ensure that you have told your reader everything, no more and no less, than is required. Second, think about the **tone** of what you write. Your writing may well be addressed to people who do not know you, and the tone says a lot about you.

Third, keep your **readers** clearly in mind. How do you feel about them? What exactly are you trying to tell them? It may be straightforward information you are offering, or you may be trying to express how you feel about something. In any event, the language must be precise and appropriate. Try to imagine yourself into the position of your audience, that is on the receiving end of what you have written, and ask yourself how they are likely to react.

Fourth, be clear about your **intention**. Is what you write intended to tell somebody something, to persuade others to adopt a point of view or to convey emotion? Anything which does not contribute to achieving the intention should be <u>cut out</u>. And as you build, turning ideas into language, it helps to look at what you have just written and ask some questions:

- Is it clear?
- Could it be clearer?
- Can I make it clearer?
- What has that last sentence added?
- Can I cut out any words without losing meaning?
- Have I said what I wanted to say?

However clear you are about these considerations, you may meet technical difficulties. It is important to avoid **ambiguity**. A sentence may be grammatically correct but say the wrong thing. For example, 'The cars were both speeding and out of control', and 'Both [the] cars were speeding and out of control', are two statements which contain the same words, but in a different order and, therefore, say different things. And the first is ambiguous. The reader may be left asking how many cars were involved, two or more?

Equally important is **exactness**. It may not matter in everything you write, but there are many occasions when the reader needs precise information. A documentary film-maker told a politician that a requested interview would take three or four minutes. 'Which?' asked the politician. 'Three or four?' *The Principles* in Chapter 2 and *The Uses* in Chapter 3 apply the same rigour. You can – and this book is designed to help – stay out of grammatical trouble, yet still be yourself.

When you have finished writing, it is time to start editing and rewriting:

- Is everything as clear as it could be?
- Does the way I write suggest I know what I am talking about?
- Can I cut out any (unnecessary) words?
- How can this be made even better?

When you leave building a wall, you can return and resume where you left off – nothing will have changed. But when you leave a piece of writing, you return to find something different; some of your former ideas may have been abandoned or reshuffled; you may try alterations or you may discard the whole thing. Writing goes on in your head even when you are away from your desk and computer.

Professional writers often use editors to look over what they have written and suggest improvements and refinements. Such editors can play a role. But most people do not have access to their services and have to be their own editors. In rewriting, you must be as critical and rigorous as they would be.

As a final check, it can help to read aloud what you have written. Although speaking style and writing style may not be exactly alike, reading aloud will show up unnatural and awkward phrases, sentences which are too long or ugly, word order which confuses, thoughts which go nowhere or are incomplete and jokes which fall flat.

The Principles of Clear English which follows is a checklist for writers. *The Uses of Clear English* covers specific points and highlights words which need special care. And *Clear Grammar and Punctuation* is a reference list to clarify definitions.

2. The Principles of Clear English: How to think and write

—

When we write, we have something to say. We have an attitude to what we have to say. We have an attitude to the people we are addressing. And we have an idea of why we are writing. Clear expression means being clear about each of these matters: sense, tone, feeling and intention. What am I saying? What do I think about it? What will they think about it? And what am I trying to do? We can start close at hand.

There is a card on this desk, typed on an old Royal typewriter. It lists George Orwell's maxims for the writing of clear English from his essay 'Politics and the English Language', published in 1946:

- Never use a metaphor, simile or other figure of speech which you are used to seeing in print.
- Never use a long word where a short one will do.
- If it is possible to cut out a word, always cut it out.
- Never use the passive where you can use the active.
- Never use a foreign phrase, a scientific word, or a jargon word if you can think of an everyday English equivalent.
- Break any of these rules sooner than say anything outright barbarous.

Orwell's maxims work. Follow them, and your writing will be sharper and clearer. However, there are some areas outside Orwell's concern which are important to those who write essays, reports, letters and briefs.

Clear writing comes from clear thinking. The better you know your subject, the better you convey it to others. The converse holds true: weak, muddled thinking produces confused writing. You are judged not only by <u>what</u> you write but by <u>how</u> you write. The best writers have a style which is at the same time their own and everyone's: clear, lucid and individual. We write to achieve things: to convey facts, to persuade someone of something, to argue a case, to outline a proposal or to propose an outline. In using language, we express ourselves and put over something of our character. If others have a view of you only from what you write, they will base their opinion on your style: clear or unclear, brief or wordy, precise or sloppy, upbeat or downbeat. Every choice of word and phrase affects their view of you. Style is who we are. As the French philosopher Pascal wrote: 'When we see a natural style, we are quite surprised and delighted, for we expected to see an author and we find a man.'

There is help. Silent rules, like rules of fashion or behaviour, have evolved to guide everyone who writes. These are the unwritten rules of appropriateness which guide us towards the style and form which suit our purpose. If you are clear about what those rules are and when they apply, your writing will be lucid and apt; if not, expect disaster. For example, a leading article from *The Economist* and a 14-line poem by Shakespeare share qualities of argument and construction but little else; you would as soon persuade a university professor of your view of Chaos Theory by writing a limerick as you would delight the delegates at a limerick festival by offering them a treatise on Chaos.

The more abstract our view of communication, the easier it becomes to see all communication as the same. But when we look at details, we see that there are many ways of saying what we mean depending on where and when we are saying it.

The principles which follow amount to plain common sense about writing. None is difficult in itself. But, just as the answers to simple questions vary throughout life, so the application of these principles varies from one writer and audience to another. Remember that writing is a means of conveying your thoughts to others; language changes, and with it the means of expression open to you; the principles of clear statement apply to planning, thinking, attitude, expression and ability to know yourself. We have listed them under: 1. Planning, 2. Thinking, 3. Communicating, 4. Writing, 5. Rewriting and 6. Ending.

1. PLANNING

1. Start before you start. Planning is a particular kind of focused thinking. Think clearly about what you will write. Know what you want to say, who you want to say it to, how you will say it and what you want to achieve by saying it.

2. Blank is good. A blank page or screen is the best feeling in the world: you can write anything you want. You have a fresh start every time you sit down to a bright new page. You can start anywhere. Just start. You can always rewrite, especially if you use a computer or word processor; you can add, move or cut anything you want. A blank screen or clean white paper should make you elated with possibility.

3. Work from an appropriate plan: if you are writing a report or an essay, give it an introduction, an argument and a conclusion;

7

if you are writing a difficult letter of condolence, write what you feel; in a business letter or essay or report, write clear, accurate English which will impress the reader with your clear, accurate mind.

4. Think of writing an introduction, a body that develops your introduction and a conclusion that supports your thesis. If you are writing an essay or report, be clear what you are writing about:
- State the problem or question.
- Gather your evidence for and against.
- Look at the evidence.
- Assess the quality of the evidence.
- Weigh the evidence.
- Conclude.

If you are replying to a letter, the tried formula works well:
- Acknowledge the last letter.
- Address the points that letter raised.
- Add your information.
- Raise questions.

If you are writing a report, remember the use of boxes, charts, columns and lists to convey your information. Using PCs has made easier the logical arrangement of information and ideas. The list is a particularly useful tool: from the shopping-list to the telephone book, the list can order information by priority, by alphabet, by urgency, by importance and so on.

5. A bad first draft is no failure; a bad first draft is a successful move on from nothing at all.

6. Order your thoughts into a logical sequence. This is not a rehearsal for what you really want to say. Say what you intend from the start.

2. THINKING

1. What you write should reflect what you think, but not necessarily in the order your thoughts occurred to you. If you are writing a love letter or a stream of consciousness novel, there is no problem. But if you are writing a report, an essay, or a structured argument, you need to make an outline before you write.

2. Base your thinking and writing on paragraphs. They are units of thought and of composition. Divide your essay or letter into its constituent topics and give a paragraph to each. The reader should be aware that you are moving on to fresh work when you start a new paragraph.

3. Within each paragraph, be consistent in the order in which words appear. Make contrasts using the same construction: 'We are more pained by ignorance than delighted by instruction,' or 'The disturbers of our happiness in this world are our desires, our griefs, and our fears; and to all these, the consideration of mortality is a certain and adequate remedy.' When you are weighing evidence, make your language balance the ideas it conveys: 'He is lazy but efficient, forgetful but thoughtful, scatty but clever,' or 'On the one hand, sales have fallen; on the other, profit has risen.' Put similar ideas in the same form: 'I have been to Ecuador, to Peru and to Colombia,' and '. . . the Ecuadoreans, the Peruvians and the Colombians'.

9

4. An ordered mind produces ordered ideas. Leave the experimental writing to James Joyce and Jack Kerouac. Or write a novel. It is hard to represent disorder without looking disordered yourself. Remember why you are writing: to make a case, report a sequence of events, to make something happen.

5. When you have a case to make, an argument to outline or a point to press, remember that unclear writing will reflect your unclear thinking.

6. Direct your argument towards reaching the proper conclusion; your argument may be valid but your conclusion irrelevant, and vice versa. If you are writing a legal brief, you need not argue that murder is horrible; but you may need to convince that the defendant has committed murder. If you are writing an essay or report, you need not say how interesting the question is or how excellent your company is; you need to answer the question or address the report.

7. Work from facts. In making a case, do not appeal to emotions or bluster: 'No intelligent, right-thinking woman could possibly believe that the earth is round.' Really? Introduce evidence as evidence and make it count for you.

8. Do not use force to make your points. 'The so-called theories of Einstein are merely the ravings of a mind polluted with liberal, democratic nonsense, which is utterly unacceptable to German men of science' (Cerf & Navasky, *The Experts Speak*, 1984, p. 300). Scientific theory should be judged by scientific evidence.

9. Do not make a case by raising questions. 'Has the company stopped selling illegal products to the developing world?' supposes a set of questions and answers which have gone before. Philosophical posturing such as 'what do we mean by history?' or 'what exactly is a management working party?' are mental wheel-spinning.

10. Do not appeal to expert evidence as the only source of truth: remember there is always an expert on each side in court, both confident, both paid. Remember, 'they all laughed at Christopher Columbus when he said the world was round, they all laughed when Edison recorded sound'.

11. Do not muddle causes and effects. One thing does not cause another because it predates it. 'The tree fell over when I made some tea' does not mean each time I have tea a tree will fall. 'A dog is an animal. A cat is an animal. Therefore a dog is a cat' is a circular argument which reaches a wrong conclusion. 'Brazil has a great soccer team. He plays for Brazil. He must be a great player,' and 'Brazil has a soccer team with outstanding players. It must be an outstanding team,' are both statements which make unreliable assumptions. It ignores the fact that good teams may include not-so-good players and that out-standing players may not constitute an outstanding team. 'All teenagers are potential delinquents. You are a teenager, so you are a potential delinquent,' makes an accusation that seems logical but may well be unjustified. Try instead: 'Some teenagers are delinquents. You are a teenager. You might be a delinquent.' Do not get carried away: an increase in paper costs may lead to a rise in the price of books, which may in turn deter people from

11

buying them. But it will not necessarily lead to the closure of all libraries, widespread illiteracy, civil war and the fall of nations.

12. Know what forms arguments commonly take, and what it is to construct one. Law, mathematics and philosophy are the best sources of pure argument. Valid arguments come in many forms; but remember that an argument may look logically valid and consistent but still be nonsensical in the real world. Here are six common forms of hypothetical argument based on the idea that if one thing happens, another follows:

1   If A, then B.
    A.
    Therefore B.

    If we oil the lock, we can open the door.
    We have oiled the lock.
    Therefore we can open the door.

This is a valid argument, even though you can imagine any number of ways of opening the door: with a chisel, with a truck and so on.

2.   If A, then B.
     Not B.
     Therefore not A.

     If we oil the lock, we can open the door.
     We cannot open the door.
     Therefore we have not oiled the lock.

This too is a valid argument, although there may be many other reasons why the door might not open; we are interested only in the relation between oiling the lock and opening the door, and not in any guesswork about whether the door is bolted, false, too heavy and so on. Like the first example, this example is always valid; and if the premises A and B are true, the conclusion must then also be true.

3   If A, then B.
    B.
    Therefore A.

    If we oil the lock, we can open the door.
    We can open the door.
    Therefore we have oiled the lock.

This is an invalid argument. It does not follow that we must have oiled the lock because we can now open the door. It could have been opened for us, or fallen open and so on.

4   If A, then B.
    Not A.
    Therefore not B.

    If we oil the lock, we can open the door.
    We have not oiled the lock.
    Therefore we can not open the door.

This too is an invalid argument, even though you can imagine any number of ways of not opening the door: we are distracted by something else, we decide not to and so on. Like the third example, this example is always invalid; and even if the premises A and B are true, the conclusion is not certain to be true.

Any of these forms of argument can be made simple and specific by saying 'If and only if A, then B'. But this reduces them to statements of fact rather than stages in an argument.

13

5   If A, then B.
    If B, then C.
    Therefore if A, then C.

    If we grow corn, we will exhaust the soil.
    If we exhaust the soil, our living will suffer.
    Therefore if we grow corn, our living will suffer.

This is a valid hypothetical syllogism. It uses three terms and makes links between them.

6   Either A or B.
    Not A.
    Therefore B.

    Either I am a man or a fish.
    I am not a man.
    Therefore I am a fish.

This is logically valid but practically nonsensical. Another example: 'Either she is a fraud or a hero. She is not a fraud. Therefore she is a hero.'

Look out for valid and invalid arguments in your writing and in others'. Rules for logical validity can be technical and bewildering. Many arguments come as statements of fact rather than – in these examples – hypotheses about the world. Here are some statements of fact, four valid and one invalid:

No soldiers are pacifists.
All Quakers are pacifists.
No Quakers are soldiers. (valid)

All polite people are kind.
Some drivers are not polite.
Some drivers are not kind. (invalid, because 'some' does not include 'all')

14

All mountaineers are brave.
No brave person is reckless.
No mountaineer is reckless. (valid)

All ruminants have horns.
All cows are ruminants.
All cows have horns. (valid)

All polite people are kind.
No parking warden is polite.
No parking warden is kind. (valid)

Often, a question about an argument comes in the form 'How do you know that?' or 'Why is that the case?' For further reading, try the classic logic textbook, *A System of Logic*, by J.S. Mill or *A Modern Elementary Logic*, by L.S. Stebbing.

13. Be wary of generalizations. Support your statements or ideas with examples, reasons, facts or similar details. As you piece a report, essay or letter together, be aware of using words of argument like 'all', 'some', 'always', 'never', 'if', 'then', 'so' and 'therefore'. To be clear about each sentence means you have to be clear about the world you are representing by writing. Think first.

3. COMMUNICATING

1. Know your audience. Who are you writing to and why? What is the purpose of your statement and why would it interest your audience? Do not try to imagine a large, massed audience. It does not exist. You are writing for an individual, or for many individuals, and not a political or religious convention, which would require a different approach to style. A note for the pedantic: while 'Whom are you writing to?' or even 'To whom are you writing?' looks grammatically correct, it is simply not our style.

2. In your attitude, write for the reader; in your craft, for yourself. For example, you should ask of your audience, 'Will this make sense to engineers?' but you should ask of yourself, 'Have I expressed this as clearly as possible?' In a sense, you have to develop and recognize your true voice and then use it to speak to your intended audience.

3. An unspoken contract exists between you and your reader. You promise not to waste time and trees, and the reader promises to give you a measure of attention and wakefulness. Anticipate questions and answer them before the reader asks them. You can help yourself and your reader by signalling the form of communication between you. Is it a memo, a sales report, a new business proposal or an essay? Let the context shape what you say: be bold enough to write 'Memo', 'Sales Report', 'Proposal' or to write out the title of the essay. Never write an account of a ferry disaster in rhyming slang.

4. Respect your reader. Show enough respect to write plain and clear English. Avoid too many words, but also too few. Try to be yourself, natural and lucid, and imagine your reader as intelligent but uninformed. Present yourself and your ideas in a way that informs your reader.

5. Never take your audience for granted. Define clearly any unfamiliar subject or concept. Writers who convey technical information face the task of representing years of experience or wisdom in a few paragraphs. How much technical information are you putting across, and how much jargon?

You are writing about, say, copper ore for the general reader. If you use the word 'dioptase', make it clear that you are writing about a particular kind of copper ore known as 'emerald copper ore'. Then say something about it. But if you are writing a specialized mining report aimed at miners, you can assume a level of expertise in the readers and count on them knowing that dioptase is translucent copper silicate, that it crystallizes in six-sided prisms, and that it is popularly known as emerald copper ore. Another example: the word 'beam' will mean one thing to a gymnast, another to an engineer, another to a particle physicist; recognize the differences.

The same principle applies to biology, computing, philosophy, physics and so on. Never assume that your reader has a necessary and sufficient knowledge of DNA, graphic interfaces or relativity. Give enough information to allow a technical word to work in the terms of your writing. The more specialized the audience, the more technical shortcuts you can take. The safest way takes an accepted fact known to all of your audience; establish that fact, and work from there.

6. Do not try to be jaunty or fashionable; it is fine if you are among friends on the Internet or informal office E-Mail, but not when you are representing yourself to the rest of the world through what you write; use regular spelling, too.

7. Avoid being pompous, or stuffy, or smug, or full of yourself or condescending. There is always someone smarter or better informed than you out there.

8. Keep a steady and consistent tone. To use slang one minute and formal language the next sends mixed messages to your readers. To be everywhere is to be nowhere; avoid trying to be all things to all.

17

9. Never be tame or tepid. Avoid vague, ill-defined words such as 'could', 'maybe', 'seems', 'might' or 'may', where uncertainty is inappropriate; be particularly careful where uncertainty could lead to ambiguity. 'The new firm could be up and running to replace the old company in a month' fails because 'could be up and running' lacks precision; whether the new <u>will</u> replace the old, and whether that <u>will</u> happen in a month is left unclear. If you can, be clear and positive.

10. Assume that you are competing for the reader's attention. Your enemies are drowsiness and the delights of elsewhere. Gently remind the reader that your essay or report will come to an end. When you start, say what you are going to do; if you are finishing, say so. Think of these things as scaffolding: 'In this report I show that homeopathic medicine is most effective in vegetarians who meditate' or 'I will first outline the sales figures, then analyse them, then make recommendations'. If saying what you are going to do, doing it and then telling the reader what you have done seems pedestrian, think again: some of the world's smartest public speakers use that formula and it is just as effective in writing.

11. Keep yourself in the background. Avoid unconventional spelling, eccentric punctuation and wild language. Be consistent. Have confidence. Your character and point of view will show.

12. Remember readers are not mind readers. Never assume what they must know. After all, married couples of twenty-five years' standing can end up having therapy because they have not been clear about what they want from each other. If someone else <u>needs</u> to know a fact, an opinion or a feeling, it is up to you to convey it.

18

13. Make sure the subject is clear. If you are wr
than one subject, let it always be clear which
discussing. An example of muddled expression
II of Schedule I to the United Kingdom Natio
(1965):

> For the purposes of this Part of this Schedule a person over
> pensionable age, not being an insured person, shall be treated as
> an employed person if he would be an insured person were he
> under pensionable age and would be an employed person were he
> an insured person.

Fine . . . if you are a civil servant paid to be puzzled about it.
Several shorter sentences might be better than a single sentence
of 49 words.

14. Imagine how you would make your point if you were
speaking to your audience. Try reading your sentences aloud;
do they sound like you? Would you find yourself saying, 'With
reference to yours of the 3rd inst.' rather than 'Thank you for
your letter'? Does this critic talk as he writes?

> Journalistic-scientific actuality-reportage fails to scan abstract-
> material hyper-objects, screening out real cyberspace emergence,
> as it comes at us out of 'front end' netware from the near future,
> invading the CNS by tuning it through biofeedback to the plane of
> neuro-electronic consistency.

This means: 'Journalists and scientists have ignored technology.' The writer can manage only garbled jargon because he has
neither clarified nor explained his thinking. The result is lazy,
pretentious and insulting to the reader. How would this writer
ask for a train ticket, or thank someone for a favour? Others try
harder; here is a computer architect falling into hectoring
simplicity:

19

e should hope that cyberspace does not turn out to be some arid domain of interaction . . . In the space between building the buildings and letting the buildings build themselves is where the new form of spatial construction can truly begin. But for that to happen we will need, quite literally, to think again.

The give-away words are 'truly' and 'quite literally'. The writer has attempted to rein in the material by shouting at us in the last two sentences. He would be clearer had he kept control.

4. WRITING

1. Ask of every sentence: What am I trying to say? What words will best express it? What image will make it clearer? And, is the image fresh enough to have an effect?

2. Always write in a way that comes naturally with words you know and trust: if you need new words, use a thesaurus or dictionary.

3. What a word means is not always what it means to you. What a word says is not what it does. A word may mean different things to different people. We see and feel the world differently. We find words from many places and we apply them to our world. But your world is not the same as your neighbour's or boss's or professor's or spouse's or children's; above all, your world is not the same as the dictionary maker's. What a word means in your dictionary is not always the same as what it means to you. Most of the time, this matters little: we generally understand what 'computer' or 'table' or 'to win' mean. But what does 'family' mean to a Mafia boss and an anthropologist? Does 'freedom' mean the same to a British Socialist and a Chinese

20

dissident? Is 'development' the same to a US oil executive and to a Warouni chief in the oil-rich Amazon?

4. What words mean is what they <u>denote</u>; what they mean to us is what they <u>connote</u>. The denotations of a word are its meaning in the dictionary; its connotations are its meanings in life. For example, **Childhood** is: 'The state or stage of life of a child; the time during which one is a child; the time from birth to puberty' (*Oxford English Dictionary*, 1971);

'State or time of being a child' (*American College Dictionary*, 1963);

'Child's state; time from birth to puberty' (*Concise Oxford Dictionary*, 1963);

'State or period of being a child' (*Oxford Dictionary of Current English*, 1985);

'The condition of being a child; the period of life before puberty' (*Collins English Dictionary of the English Language*, 1986);

'*Her childhood* = the time when she was a child' (*Cambridge International Dictionary of English*, 1995);

'The condition or period of being a child' (*Oxford Advanced Learner's Dictionary*, 1995);

'When I was young and my parents took me to the beach . . .' (Your definition).

Do the compilers of these dictionaries know more about what childhood means to you than you do? Do they know about its connotations for you? No. But have they evolved a generally accepted meaning? Do they know what the word 'childhood' denotes? Yes. As you write, remember that your experience of the world differs from other people's; men and women have gone to war over less.

21

5. Use words to build strong, logical sentences. Nothing is so elusive as the perfect sentence.

6. Sentences perform many duties, and follow many patterns. Think about your sentences in terms of grammar, use, and the order of words and clauses.

7. What kinds of sentences are there?

Simple sentences have one clause containing one finite verb and one predicate.

Robert drank beer.

The sentence can remain simple even if we add some modifiers.

My thirsty cousin Robert noisily drank a tankard of beer before going to bed.

Despite the enlargement, there is still only one finite verb, *drank*, therefore there can only be one clause.

Jack decided to give his last few coins to the local hospice fund.

This sentence has only one clause, one subject (*Jack*), one finite verb (*decided*) and one predicate (the rest of the sentence). But this time, within the predicate, there is a direct object (*coins*) and an indirect object (*the local hospice fund*).

Simple sentences are independent (main) clauses. They make sense on their own.

Compound sentences comprise two or more main clauses, each having a subject and a predicate containing a finite verb, and each making sense when standing alone. The clauses are linked by the conjunctions, 'and', 'but', 'or' or 'nor'; or by a colon or a semicolon.

He returned to New York and drove to an apartment near Central Park.

They have been digging the well in the middle of the field, <u>but</u> they have not struck water yet.

Speech is silver: silence is golden.

Complex sentences are made up of one main clause and one or more dependent (subordinate) clauses, none of which would make sense on its own.

Just before midnight, thirty landing craft cast off in silence from the towing boats that had brought them across the Channel.

There are only two finite verbs (*cast off* and *had brought*) and therefore only two clauses. The first, *Just . . . boats*, is the <u>main</u> clause with *that . . . Channel* as the <u>subordinate</u> clause. The latter cannot stand alone and is <u>dependent</u> on the former for its meaning.

Compound-complex sentences are a mixture of the two types, that is with two or more <u>main</u> clauses and one or more <u>subordinate</u> clauses.

As I <u>was awakened</u> by the dawn chorus, I <u>took</u> an early breakfast and <u>had</u> time to walk to the station.

The first clause is <u>subordinate</u>. The other two are <u>main</u>. Finite verbs are underlined.

Incomplete sentences have no verb and are fragments. They are informal, and are widely and correctly used, particularly in conversation. Examples include *So far, so good. My pleasure. Now, to the facts. Of course. No comment. Sorry about that.*

Incomplete sentences can have a powerful effect in writing provided they are not over-used.

Six o'clock. Three hours. Nick should have returned an hour ago. He was stiff with waiting. Laurels over to his right jerked and settled. Only the wind. Or should he have looked more closely?

23

Using sentences

A **declarative** sentence can be used to make an assertion, which may be positive or negative.

Shakespeare was born in 1564 and died in 1616.

It is not the case that all great writers are vegetarians.

An **interrogative** sentence is used to ask a question.

Is there anything interesting on television this evening?

Why don't the leaves on the clipped beech hedges fall in the autumn?

An **imperative** sentence issues a command or expresses a request.

Get that dog out of this room at once.

Give me all that you owe me and I will trouble you no more.

An **exclamatory** sentence expresses a strong reaction, such as surprise, distress, elation and so on.

What a tragedy! To be assassinated by a maniac!

O, what a noble mind is here o'erthrown.

So near the shore and not a soul saved. Incredible!

Ordering words and clauses

In English, the normal word order in a sentence is subject – verb – object – complement.

He climbed the mountain in winter.

Sentences which follow this order are called <u>loose</u>. When the verb is held back until the end, they are called <u>periodic</u>. How we use loose and periodic sentences affects our writing style.

Most of us talk using **loose sentences**. We find them naturally shaped, easy to understand, and we don't have to wait until the sentence is complete to know what happened. The main points of what is being conveyed appear in the early part of the loose sentence. Details and elaborations are added later, phrase by phrase and clause by clause.

The rally car coughed her way back into the garage with her two-man crew completely exhausted, her bodywork hidden by mud and debris, her windscreen opaque and cracked after the contest with the punishing roads, streams and mountain winds.

The important element here is the car's return to its base (*The rally car . . . garage*). The rest of the sentence describes the condition of the crew, the state of the car and the weather, in a straightforward progression, one thing following another. These could have been put in a different order if the writer had wished. This sentence could have ended at several points (*garage, exhausted, debris, cracked, winds*) and would still have made sense. Another example of a loose sentence is:

She was eminently well-suited to judge this competition as she was a practical, independent-minded woman not dazzled by surface glitter or bewildered by the latest fads and fashions.

In a **periodic sentence**, the most important piece of information is held back until the end to create a movement of growing force. The meaning is only complete when the end is reached.

It is not what he has, nor even what he does, which unmistakably shows the worth of a man, but what he is.

Although I am accounted successful, and some think that I am rich, there are times that occur if I am alone when I grieve over my unhappiness.

In a **mixed sentence**, the individual writer can express his or her own style. The most important information may appear anywhere in the sentence order.

Although the ground is hard with frost, I shall go to meet her on foot, whatever you say or think.

Style is improved and is more interesting when the writer uses a variety of sentence types. Examine your own writing to see what you tend to do. None of us finds it difficult to write loose sentences; they come naturally. But if, for variety, you want to write a periodic sentence, or to make a loose sentence periodic, it is quite simple. All you need to do is put modifying phrases or clauses first and reserve a position near the end for the verb.

The soldiers made good headway through the narrow pass and overcame opposition as it appeared even though they were many fewer now and most were exhausted.

is a loose sentence which can be turned into a periodic sentence like this:

Although many fewer now, and mostly exhausted, the soldiers overcame opposition and made good headway through the narrow pass.

A **balanced sentence** is a stylistic arrangement in which two or more assertions produce a satisfying tension when brought together. Proverbs and wise sayings often show close parallelisms in thought and grammatical structure.

To err is human; to forgive, divine.
He who excuses himself, accuses himself.
Marry in haste; repent at leisure.

Although grammatical parallelism may be present, balance is not dependent on it. Rather, the different parts of the sentence are carefully shaped so that they help achieve the rhythm and unity which the writer wants.

They not only went into his orchard and stole the apples, but they knocked at his door to ask for bags to put them in.

8. Strip every sentence to its bones; that is the trick of good writing. Aim for clarity and simplicity. Use a short word rather than risk confusion with a long one. If you are uncertain of a word's meaning, do not use it. This is no time to try out new words or structures. This is a time to be yourself.

9. Write with nouns and verbs. Use adjectives and adverbs sparingly. 'Hydrogen and oxygen ions combine to form water' conveys information more aptly than 'Hydrogen ions operating in pairs ambush and attack unsuspecting lone oxygen ions and force them into an uneasy alliance to form water'. Too many adverbs and adjectives spell weak writing. Adverbs, like adjectives, take force and vigour from what they qualify: clauses like 'accelerate quickly', 'smashed hard' or 'plummeted swiftly' not only look sloppy, they also weaken the verb and make you appear to be trying too hard.

10. Stick to existing words. There are over 300,000 entries in the *Oxford English Dictionary*, although many are obsolete. In practice, the *Concise Oxford Dictionary*, with over 63,000 entries, should give you all the words you need. Oxford linguists think that the vocabulary of an educated native English speaker lies in the range 50,000–250,000 words. This range makes the 1,000 words we use for about three quarters of our daily business seem small. Read dictionaries and thesauruses ('thesauri' for the pedantic). Embrace new words; use them but do not be used by them.

The words we use tend to be current and familiar. Words such as 'bimbo' (1988 but in use in the USA since 1900), 'cyberspace' (1984), 'hacker' (1960), 'modem' (1980), 'new world order' (1990), 'quantum leap' (1970), 'rubbish' (verb, 1972), 'turbo' (1986) and 'yuppie' (1984) came from the last thirty years and have entered the language. Words such as 'dynamic', 'global', 'happening', 'holistic', 'radical' or 'weird' had a vogue in the 1980s and are still beating at the covers of the dictionaries to claim renewed meaning. But there is a difference between current and standard words.

11. Negatives muddy a clear sentence. Where possible, avoid •
them. 'He was impressed by our argument' is a stronger statement
than 'He was not unimpressed by our argument'. Introducing a
negative into what is a positive statement gives the words a
different meaning. The first example above is a straightforward
assertion without qualification; the second makes a similar
statement but is softened by the negative. The implication is
that, while 'He' was not left totally unmoved by what we said,
he was not necessarily terribly impressed by it either.

Wherever possible, positive statements should be unequi-
vocal. Negatives can suggest a doubt, introduce a note of irony
or simply 'hold back'.

12. Be clear about the subjects of each sentence. Use shorter
sentences if you feel out of control; you will make fewer
diversions into other territory. This science writer, for example, is trying to say too much in one sentence:

*One of the great discoveries of twentieth-century science, the fact
of continental movement as a result of plate tectonics, puts history
in a new light, one that is very difficult for human minds, so much
in the thrall of the present, to understand.*

This translates as: 'The twentieth-century discovery of the
movement of continents offers us a new view of history. We
might find this view hard to grasp because we look so much to the
present.' The writer has allowed excitement over the material to
cloud judgement of the order of ideas in the sentence.

13. Keep the subject at the front of the reader's attention. The
subject of your sentence is the main issue. It is why you wrote
the sentence in the first place. The line 'Hell hath no fury like a
woman scorned' gathers hell, fury, woman and scorn into a
strong unit. Try expressing this differently but as effectively.

Here are a few weaker possibilities:

Fury-wise in hell, the scorned woman is top.

How furious a scorned woman can be!

There is nothing more furious in hell than the fury of a scorned woman.

In terms of scorned women, there is no fury in hell more furious.

14. At the end of every paragraph ask: Has this paragraph addressed the subject? Is it vital? If not, can I cut it out?

15. Get to the point. If you look at any newspaper, you will see that the headline is written to grab our attention, and the essentials of the story are contained in the first couple of paragraphs. Readers of every type of writing are looking, consciously or subconsciously, for the answers to basic questions – who, what, where, how, why, when? The most effective statement is the one which leaves none of these questions unanswered.

Elmore Leonard's novel, *Split Images*, opens with these words:
In the winter of 1981, a multimillionaire by the name of Robinson Daniels shot a Haitian refugee who had broken into his home in Palm Beach.

From this we know who (Robinson Daniels, a multimillionaire), what and how (shot a Haitian refugee), where (at his home in Palm Beach), why (the Haitian had broken into his home) and when (winter 1981).

Book One of George Eliot's *Middlemarch* opens like this:
Miss Brooke had that kind of beauty which seems to be thrown into relief by poor dress.

This one sentence not only gives us who but establishes Miss Brooke as a central character in the story and tells us quite a lot about her.

16. Be exact. Many types of writing require quantities, percentages, etc. to be stated precisely. A lot can be at stake if there is ambiguity or uncertainty. In the last forty years, the average contract relating to the sale of a private business has grown from about twelve to over one hundred pages. But more general writing can also be a minefield. In some contexts, exactness may not seem to matter, but when a writer refers to 'the vast majority', does that amount to 90% or 80% or perhaps 76.5%? While it may not be necessary to put an exact figure on it, this kind of vague numerical reference lays the writer open to challenge and undermines what is written. Such terminology should be used with the greatest care and, if in doubt, avoided.

100% all
96–100% almost all
90–96% vast majority
75–90% great majority
53–75% majority
47–53% about half
30–50% a substantial part
20–30% a significant part
6–20% a material part
1–6% a small part
less than 1% a very small amount

17. Be consistent in the use of names, titles, places, dates and times. Use a spellcheck program on your computer or run a name-change program: 'Miss Green' on page 1 should not become 'Ms Green' on page 2. Where you can, find out if local rules apply; for example, 'chair' for 'chairman' or 'Ms' for 'Miss' or 'access cover' for 'manhole' and so on. You are responsible for spelling proper names correctly.

18. Be exact about time. Accuracy means accuracy about time, too. Make clear by using verb tenses when something happens, will happen or is expected to happen, and when something has already happened:

The new hospital will house 1,000 medical students; some will have qualified as doctors when the building opens; others will have had to retake their exams and will still be waiting for their results.

If in doubt, draw a line diagram with the present in the middle and the distant past and distant future extending to the left and right. Then mark in the events you are describing. If you need to use flow diagrams in your essay or presentation or report, use them.

19. Never overwrite or overstate or overqualify: 'almost nearly perfectly flat' means 'nearly flat' and 'there was a massive crash in the UK stock market in October 1987' means 'the stock market fell a particular number of points on a specific day in October 1987'.

20. Try to use the active voice where you can. 'Jane and Simon and I had a meeting last week' is better than 'A meeting was convened last week with Jane and Simon and me' just as 'I will remember my first tennis match' is better than 'my first tennis match will always be remembered by me'. Verbs work the sentence. Keep the sentence full of energy by making them active; try to cut 'to be' wherever possible. Instead of 'the new proposals were deemed to be an insult to the management', write 'the new proposals insulted the management'. Active sentences, with a subject and an object, give more information than passive forms.

21. Where you think you may need a passive, check exactly what you want to say. Are you really saying 'Our software programs are highly regarded this year'? Or are you saying

'Some people in the industry now think well of our software'? Choose 'Ill health forced him to resign' over 'The reason he resigned was because he succumbed to ill health'.

22. Avoid ambiguity. 'Her approachability set her apart', 'She's a staggering dancer' and 'I will waste no time in reading your book' look like compliments but are ambiguous. As you reread your writing, watch the tone and content. Cut concepts or words having more than one specific meaning or potentially confusing meaning.

The critic William Empson wrote a book called *Seven Types of Ambiguity* (1930) and founded an academic industry which scoured literature for multiple meanings, inadvertent words and undiscovered intentions. Sometimes phrases pack themselves with ambiguity: 'Nothing so true as what you once let fall, most women have no character at all' varies according to how you speak it. But if you write 'I saw a car with three wheels over the balcony', expect amazement.

Keep things simple to avoid ambiguity. Good writing carries energy from one sentence to the next. It is robust and direct enough to travel through the rockiest territory.

5. REWRITING

1. Write, read, rewrite, reread, rewrite. Brevity is your friend, space your ally, and time your enemy. Writing is the ability to meet the challenge of filling the available space. Remember that professional writers rewrite many times. The novelist Gustave Flaubert used to say that he never rewrote one word without having to change twelve. The triumph lies in putting some mark on the screen or page in front of you; from that moment, you are writing and rewriting, not starting. The term 'editing' means the combination of reading, judging and altering your work. It means reading your work critically and writing again those parts which are unclear, ugly or stupid. It is generally better to cut out words than to write more. Short words speak best.

2. As you rewrite, be bold enough to cut out paragraphs which do not work and to re-order the rest until they do. After you have cut or moved a passage, make sure that each paragraph – your fundamental unit of thought – still makes sense and relates to what goes before and comes after.

3. Rewriting can be going on when you are away from your desk, when you put down your pen or switch off your computer. Trust yourself. If you have a feeling that something you have written is muddled, out of place or sloppy, your nagging doubts should send you back to the writing.

4. Editing can be simple and easy but not painless. As you read and reshape what you have written, use your skills as a reader; you have been reading almost all your life, so draw on your experience and be prepared to delete anything that looks weak or unclear.

5. Keep words and sentences as short as you can. As Mark Twain wrote, 'At time he may indulge himself with a long one, but he will make sure there are no folds in it, no vaguenesses, no parenthetical interruptions of its view as a whole; when he has done with it, it won't be a sea-serpent with half of its arches under the water; it will be a torch-light procession'. If you need a long sentence to convey your meaning, fine.

6. Check that each word or phrase matches its context. Talk about a 'car journey' rather than 'a vehicular peregrination'; prefer 'He did the job' to 'He fit the straight leg of command with the trouser of dispatch' or 'He completed the task in hand'. Do not 'proceed to the vehicle' but 'walk to the car/truck/bike'. Few constructions outside technical or legal documents need be protracted.

7. Make sure every word counts. Cut waffle or blather. Try to think of what you want to say, and say it. Avoid this:

In its intrinsic remoteness from direct human experience, Boolean search logic shows another part of the infomania syndrome: a gain in power at the price of our direct involvement with things.

This means: 'Boolean logic is powerful but remote'.

8. Avoid clichés. Conventional wisdom tends to advise against the use of clichés. A cliché is 'a phrase which has lost most of its power through overuse and which, because of its familiarity, draws attention to itself rather than to what the words say'. A well-placed cliché may entertain the reader. The *key factor* is that the reader should be in *no doubt* that the writer is aware of having used a cliché. If we seem to have *let it slip in* by accident, *we are sunk* and nobody will take what we write seriously.

9. Use specific and definite language. Writers from Shakespeare to Elmore Leonard, philosophers from Montaigne to Mill, and management theorists from Machiavelli to Peter Drucker write in concrete terms. Herbert Spencer, friend of George Eliot, showed how specific terms carry greater weight than generalization:

In proportion as the manners, customs, and amusements of a nation are cruel and barbarous, the regulations of its penal code will be severe.

In proportion as men delight in battles, bullfights, and combats of gladiators, they will punish by hanging, burning and the rack.

10. Cut out abstract nouns: 'He found himself in a no-win situation' means 'He could not win'; 'This was, for her, a vertical climbing scenario' simply means 'She was climbing'; 'Mathematical logic gained the upper hand by severing its significance from the conditions under which we make direct statements' can be shortened to 'Logic won by standing alone'. Try to avoid combining two or more abstracts: 'global cumulative turbulence', 'reversible generative stagflation' and 'gradual illusory diffusion' sound and look smart but mean little.

11. When editing, ask of every sentence: 'Is this a necessary and sufficient account of what I am thinking?' and then ask 'How can I cut out more words?' Cut out every word which fails to further your meaning or which clouds or hampers your meaning. If you know another language, try translating your English into that language and then back again. Is it simpler, clearer or cleaner? Try paraphrasing what you have written.

12. The first rule of language is that we *can* break the other rules at will. But in writing, rule breaking involves risk. Judge how great the risk is. Language changes; English is influenced by other types (e.g. American); jargon comes and goes. If writers want to express themselves more individually and vividly by breaking some of the rules, they must feel supremely confident that the effect they will have is what they intend. If your instinct tells you to doubt the wisdom of breaking the rules, it is better not to break them.

6. ENDING

1. In writing, as in life, good beginnings and endings are vital. Never leave a piece of writing unfinished. Never leave yourself or your readers dissatisfied.

2. Ending is one thing, concluding another. Conclusions have to be planned for, reached for and paid for throughout your writing. If a report or essay starts with a question, the conclusion should offer a proposition or a recommendation.

3. Know how and when you will end before you start. The French philosopher Pascal wrote: 'The last thing one knows in constructing work is what to put first.' The first thing you should know is what you will put last. You should know how you will end: and when you are ready to stop, stop. If you have followed a plan you should have written your introduction and marshalled your arguments; now you are ready to conclude. This is easy. Make sure that if the reader has been distracted or asleep, your final paragraphs give a pithy, lucid summary of your arguments; then say what you think or hope or fear will happen. Push your writing out into the world again.

4. Your conclusion will not be the last thing you write, nor your introduction the first. Computers make this easy. You can move paragraphs and sentences wherever you wish; you can hold a good idea fully or partially formed; and you can prune or graft your sentences. If you have been arguing, editing and rereading, you may have a supply of material which seemed inapposite earlier but which fits the conclusion. Use it.

5. The best endings come right like the click of a closing door. Shakespeare knew the trick:

If this be error and upon me proved,
I never writ, nor no man ever loved.

Francis Bacon mastered the exit line in his writing:

Histories make men wise; poets, witty; the mathematics, subtle;
natural philosophy, deep; moral, grave; logic and rhetoric, able
to contend.

Bacon rounded up his arguments and made a summary of them. This can be particularly effective if the writer anticipates opposition. Charles Darwin wrote, in the conclusion to his *The Descent of Man* (1871):

> The main conclusion arrived at in this work, namely that man is descended from some lowly-organized form, will, I regret to think, be highly distasteful to many persons . . . [one page later he concludes] Man still bears in his bodily frame the indelible stamp of his lowly origin.

6. Use the ending to broaden the scope of what precedes it. Abraham Lincoln's Gettysburg Address (19 November 1863) summed up the American Civil War:

> . . . that we here highly resolve that these dead shall not have died in vain – that this nation, under God, shall have a new birth of freedom – and that government of the people, by the people, for the people, shall not perish from the earth.

In *The Roving Mind. A Panoramic View of Fringe Science, Technology, and the Society of the Future* (1987), the scientist Isaac Asimov used a concluding paragraph to warn:

> The good earth is dying; so in the name of humanity let us move. Let us make our hard but necessary decisions. Let us do it quickly. Let us do it now.

7. Do not shirk. Life goes on, and there are other things to read and write. Even *War and Peace* has a final line. Or as the Red Queen says in *Alice's Adventures in Wonderland*, 'Begin at the beginning and go on till you come to the end: then stop.'

3. The Uses of Clear English:
A list of clear and unclear uses

The term <u>uses</u> means the manner, treatment or application of specific problems in clear style, encountered in all areas of writing. This chapter lists alphabetically words and phrases whose meaning is sometimes unclear, or which may be confused with other words and phrases, and gives examples of correct usage with explanations where appropriate.

a, an, the
<u>A</u>, <u>an</u> and <u>the</u> are called articles; <u>a</u> and <u>an</u> are indefinite articles (the reader does not know specifically what is being written about): <u>the</u> is the definite article (the reader knows what is being referred to).

The basic difference between <u>a</u> and <u>an</u> is that <u>a</u> is used in front of words which begin with a consonant or a pronounced 'u', as in *a year, a unit* (but not *an umbrella*); <u>an</u> is used in front of a word or an abbreviation which begins with a vowel or a vowel sound, and also before a silent 'h', as in *an armchair, an M.P., an honour* (but not *a harvest*). <u>A</u> and <u>an</u> are used before singular countable nouns, as in *a good suggestion, an umbrella*; <u>the</u> is used before specific singular or plural countable nouns, as in

The milkman forgot our order.

Turn off the lights please.

and *the police, the army, the girls*.

Sometimes <u>the</u> is used before uncountable nouns, as in *the music, the weather*. But <u>a</u> and <u>an</u> can never be used before an uncountable noun.

If a sentence requires *a* and *an*, both must be used:

He is an officer and a gentleman.

see **loose sentences**; **nouns**

accustomed

Accustomed is used in three ways. It is an adjective meaning 'customary, what is generally done' and is followed by the infinitive:

He was accustomed to go for a short walk each evening.

It is an adjective meaning 'used to, feeling compelled to' and is followed by 'to' and the gerund:

I am not accustomed to eating cooked breakfasts.

And it is a verb, followed by the gerund:

In times of severe drought, we all accustomed ourselves to fetching water from the pump.

actually

When correctly used, actually refers to contrasting notions, differences between appearance and reality, and between theory and fact:

At first it looks a difficult problem, but you will find that actually it is quite easy to solve.

I know how to collect a swarm of bees, but I have never actually had to do so.

When loosely or incorrectly used, it is often just padding and adds nothing to the meaning:

Actually, I neither smoke nor drink.

He actually had the effrontery to call me a clown.

She didn't actually impress us on first meeting.

Nothing would be lost by deleting actually from these sentences.

affinity

Traditionally, affinity has been followed by the prepositions 'between' and 'with'. These have now been joined by 'to' and 'for' which, though less common, are acceptable. Affinity exists between two people or things; we say that one has an affinity with the other:

The affinity between the two sisters was an inspiration to everyone who met them.

Caroline's affinity with Penny, and Penny's with Caroline showed the highest form of social achievement.

His feeling of affinity to Provence drew him there every year for his holiday.

The British have an affinity for dogs and other animals which is a source of bewilderment to mainland Europeans.

If in doubt, use 'between' or 'with'; take care with 'for' and avoid 'to'.

ago, for, since

These are adverbs which indicate how, when or where something happened. Ago is used after, not before, an expression of time to indicate when something happened: it is used with the past tense:

It started snowing an hour ago.

For indicates how long something lasts. It is used with present, past and future tenses:

I study French for three hours every day.

I studied French for three years.

I will study French for three months next year.

Since is used to indicate how long something has been happening. It gives the starting point of an action that continues to the present and is normally used in the present perfect tense which brings the action being described from the past up to the present:

It is years since the house was painted.

He has lived there since 1944.

When <u>since</u> is preceded by <u>ever</u>, continuity is expressed but without a specific time reference:

His health has improved ever since he gave up banking and became a market gardener.

<u>Ago</u> and <u>since</u> can never be used side by side in a sentence:

It is ten years ago since I saw him is wrong.

This should be *It was ten years ago that I saw him* or *I saw him ten years ago* or *It is ten years since I saw him.*

<u>Since</u> can also mean 'because'

see **adverbs**; **verb tenses**.

all, all of

<u>All</u> is used when a pronoun is followed by a noun in apposition, as in *all you readers, all us pensioners*; and with nouns which refer to distance, quantity, etc., as in *all the way, all the sandwiches*. It is also used without the definite article when referring to specific periods of time, as in *all day, all night, all month, all year. All of the night* is not incorrect but is unlikely to appear in everyday writing. <u>All of</u> is used before a pronoun, as in *all of you, all of them*, etc.

also

<u>Also</u> is an adverb, not a conjunction. It should not be used to open a clause or a sentence. *He works as a silversmith. Also he teaches part-time* is wrong and should be *He works as a silversmith. He also teaches part-time*. However, an exception to this rule is the placing of <u>also</u> at the beginning of a sentence for special emphasis and where it obviously follows on from the sentence before:

The family miraculously survived the explosion. Also found alive in the rubble were their two cats, still in their basket.

<u>Also</u> should not follow a comma to co-ordinate two nouns unless it is preceded by 'and' or 'but'.

She bought a pressure cooker, and also three saucepans.

Not only did she buy a pressure cooker, but also three saucepans.

see **not only . . . but (also)**

although, though

These two words are often, but not always, interchangeable.

She chose the blue coat although/though it was not the one she had meant to buy.

<u>Although</u> tends to be more formal and emphatic:

He took an uncompromising stand at the meeting, although I had warned him about the likely consequences.

<u>Although</u> is preferable to open a sentence:

Although he had been warned about the consequences, he refused to compromise.

Neither <u>although</u> nor <u>though</u> should be used to close a sentence. (*Did you invite him? Yes, he isn't coming though* is heard in informal spoken English but is not appropriate in writing.)

Particular uses of <u>though</u>, where <u>although</u> could not be used, are: after 'as' or 'even':

It was as though he had never been there.

I recognized her, even though we had never met.

as a substitute for 'but', 'yet' or 'however':

I like her though I don't think she likes me.

She is very pretty though careless about how she dresses.

among *see* **between**

and

<u>And</u> is a co-ordinating conjunction which should be used to join elements of a similar type and weight.

Dictionaries are essential for those who want to write more accurately and to speak more effectively.

Disregard the advice that a sentence should never start with <u>and</u>. It can be arresting and effective (*And I should warn you . . .*), but should be used in moderation. Over-use lessens its effectiveness and leads to too many loose sentences.

see **loose sentences**

any

As a pronoun, <u>any</u> takes a single or plural verb according to the context:

Is any of the crew missing? (That is, *Is any single member of the crew missing?*) *Are any of the crew missing?* (That is, *some, more than one*).

If no specific reference to one or more than one is intended, <u>any</u> used with 'you', 'us', 'them' etc. tends to take the plural verb:

Are any of you interested in coming?

anybody, anyone, any one

<u>Anybody</u> and <u>anyone</u> are readily interchangeable. Although each is a singular (*Is anybody/anyone coming?*), there are occasions when a plural pronoun has to be used (*Has anybody/anyone filled in their income tax form yet?*). In most cases it would not be possible to replace 'their' with 'his', 'her', 'one's', etc. Only in the most formal writing would it be preferable to think up a different way of saying things (*Has anybody/anyone filled in an income tax form yet?*).

<u>Any one</u> as two words gives a different meaning and emphasis:

Anyone could have saved him is a general statement and could have been *Anybody could have saved him.*

Any one of the onlookers could have saved him is restricted and more specific.

When referring to things, the two-word form should always be used:

Any one of these teapots will do for our picnic.

as

Used once, as may simply mean 'because' (*As you didn't meet, she will telephone you tomorrow*) or 'when/while' (*As I walked past, I saw her at the window; As I was looking through the window, it began to snow*).

When as is followed by as later in the same statement, take care to avoid errors and ambiguity.

As good as gold presents no problem; *as keen as me* is wrong (though common in speech) and should be *as keen as I* in written English.

Jennifer loves her little sister as much as me is not wrong, but what does it mean? That Jennifer loves her little sister as much as Jennifer loves me; or, that Jennifer loves her little sister as much as I love her little sister? Strictly, it means the former. To express the latter, we would have to say, *Jennifer loves her little sister as much as I* (often followed by *do*).

Susan paints portraits as well as Tom is not incorrect, but does it mean that Susan and Tom both paint portraits, or that the portraits Susan paints are as good as the ones Tom paints? It is important to be clear about which you mean and, if there is any doubt, rewrite.

As is frequently used with other common prepositions. When used with 'so', it can simply replace as . . . . as:

He is not so/as easily satisfied as he used to be.

When a negative construction precedes an infinitive verb, 'so' is preferable:

I am not so sure of myself as to celebrate before I know the results.

As is commonly used wrongly with 'from':

We are closing for minor repairs as from next Friday should be *We are closing for minor repairs from next Friday.*

Hostilities will cease as from 11th November is simply wrong and should be *Hostilities will cease on 11th November.*

The doors will be closed as from midday on bank holidays is also wrong and should be *The doors will be closed at midday on bank holidays.*

However, it is acceptable to link <u>as</u> with 'from' when making a retrospective announcement:

The agreed family allowance increase will be paid as from 1st January last year.

<u>As</u> is often used, incorrectly and unnecessarily, with 'to':

There was heated debate (as to) whether or not he should stay on.

<u>As . . . to</u> can be taken out, just as it can in:

He avoided answering the question (as to) why he had not told the police.

Sometimes a different word is needed:

They had no information as to the snow conditions should be *They had no information about the snow conditions.*

What are your thoughts as to the practicability of this expedition? should be *What are your thoughts on the practicability of this expedition?*

<u>As well as</u> introduces a parenthesis and usually means 'in addition to':

This ointment has a cleansing as well as a soothing effect.

Children, as well as adults, have specific needs.

When <u>as well as</u>, meaning 'in addition to', links clauses, the clause that follows the phrase is non-finite and takes the . . . ing form:

As well as watching Great Expectations on TV, he is reading the book.

The storm uprooted several trees as well as demolishing the garden shed.

Used carelessly, <u>as well as</u> can lead to ambiguity (*see above*).

see **though**

at, in

When indicating location, <u>at</u> is used to refer to recognized public places. It is more exclusive and specific:

I work at the town hall.
I will meet you at Harrods.
The family were living at Howards End.

<u>In</u> is more inclusive and general:

I work in an office.
I live in London.
She has gone to work in Germany.
Wouldn't you rather live in a flat?

Sometimes, in a more complex statement, it is appropriate to use both:

I live at Ilfracombe in Devon.
I live in Coronation Street at number 4.

<u>At</u> + <u>at</u> and <u>in</u> + <u>in</u> in a sentence is clumsy.

backward, backwards

There is an important difference between these two words. <u>Backward</u> is an adjective:

He is very bright, but his lack of confidence makes him backward in voicing his ideas.
Taking up that job was, unfortunately, a backward step.

<u>Backwards</u> is an adverb:

He looked backwards to see if the road was clear.
My career seems to be going backwards.

<u>Backwards</u> is sometimes used idiomatically:

I know this symphony backwards.
I leant over backwards to help her, but she wouldn't respond.
Backwards and forwards.

basically

This is an overused word, often redundant, and simply a form of padding, especially as the first word in the reply to a question or in an assertion:

Basically, I don't care for carrots.

Basically, I didn't think the book was any good at all.

In both of these, basically is meaningless and should be deleted.

Basically should not be used to open a sentence and, where it is used, it should have its literal meaning, 'fundamentally':

I think the supports are basically sound, but they have worked loose in the soft soil.

because *of see* **due to**

beg the question

To beg the question does not, as some people believe, mean to ask, raise or evade a question. It means to arrive at a conclusion by assuming the truth or validity of something which itself requires proof. Assertion is not proof.

The divisive Council Tax should be abolished does not in itself 'prove' that the Council Tax is divisive, nor does it indicate who has suggested that it is. The context is likely to require those points to be answered.

behalf

In the form 'on behalf of', the term means 'in the interests of' or 'as representative for':

The barrister put up a brilliant defence on behalf of his client.

I speak on behalf of the whole audience in thanking you for such an instructive talk this evening.

Don't be concerned on my behalf (= on account of me).

Sometimes, on behalf of is wrongly used to mean 'on the part of':

There was great reluctance on the part of (not on behalf of) the minister to answer any of the questions put to him.

beside, besides

Beside is a preposition and means 'next to', 'at the side of', 'in conjunction with':

He looked up and said, 'Would you like to sit beside me?'
Beside your earlier writing, this seems really mature.

It can also be used in a non-literal way:

He was beside himself with anger when his application was turned down.

Besides is a preposition and an adverb meaning 'in addition to', 'moreover', 'except', 'other than'. Its position in a sentence depends upon the meaning:

The book was boring besides being badly written.
Four of us besides the grandchildren are going swimming.
He has no connections with the army now besides me.
I don't like truffles and besides I can't afford such luxuries.
If you want to paint the hall, here is a paintbrush each and three others besides.

between, among

These words are used in many contexts and there is often confusion between them. The most common relates to the number of elements in a sentence. The rule is that between is used when there are two elements; and among with any number larger than two:

There have long been differences between Britain and Spain over Gibraltar.
She shared out her lottery win among her four children.

Between is used with 'and', not 'or':

You must choose between your work or your social life is wrong.

Between should not be used with 'each' or 'every':

There is a pause of one second between each wave is wrong and should be *There is a pause of one second between the waves.* Although there are certainly more than two waves, *There is a pause . . . among the waves* is wrong as the statement means that there is a pause of a second between one wave and the next one.

In everyday language, <u>between</u> is now frequently used instead of <u>among</u> where it is not specifically stated how many elements there are:

The arguments between the world's top financiers were settled last night.

The committee found the differences between them were too great to be overcome.

<u>Between</u> is also commonly used when describing a group's collective activity:

The fundraisers managed to raise £1000 between them.

and in idiomatic use:

Just between ourselves . . . referring to two or more people.

both, each

Misuse frequently leads to confusion. The following sentence is unclear:

We were both awarded a first prize could mean there were two first prizes awarded, or that we shared first prize. If the former is intended, the sentence should read *We were each awarded a first prize.* If the latter, state simply, *We shared first prize.*

In his anger, he turned on both his friends and his enemies might mean that he only had two friends. It is unclear. To avoid misunderstanding, this would be better as *In his anger he turned on friends and enemies alike.*

<u>Both</u> can only refer to two elements taken together and requires a plural verb:

Both boys went off to the races.

Both cattle and sheep are bred by those farmers.

<u>Both</u> needs 'of' in *both of us, both of you* and *both of them.*

It may often be redundant when another word does its work. Such words include 'equally', 'alike', 'between', 'identical':

Both men were equally dangerous is wrong and should be *The men were equally dangerous.*

<u>Each</u> refers to one of any number and requires a singular verb:

Each of you has (not *have*) *something to offer.*

burned, burnt

Either can be used to indicate past tense. <u>Burnt</u> is used transitively:

On graduating, he burnt all his lecture notes.

<u>Burned</u> is used intransitively:

The fire burned for several hours.

He burned with hatred at the insult to his family.

Burnt can be an adjective:

A burnt offering.

Use a little more burnt sienna.

His hands were quite badly burnt.

but

<u>But</u> is a conjunction which links and contrasts conflicting ideas. It should not be used to link elements which are in harmony, nor in a sentence with 'however' which means the same thing.

When it means 'except', <u>but</u> is followed by a subject or object, depending on its position in a sentence. The subject should be used when it comes in the middle:

The whole crowd but he were wearing scarves.

The object should be used when it comes at the end:

Everyone was there but him.

<u>But</u> may be preceded by 'everything' to mean 'except':

Everything but the kitchen sink = except the kitchen sink.

<u>But</u> may be preceded by 'nothing' to mean 'only':

We have nothing but carrots left = we have only carrots left.

<u>But</u> may be followed by 'for' to mean 'were it not for', 'had it not been for':

We would have had a bumper harvest but for the late frost.

Purists argue against starting a sentence with <u>but</u>. It can, however, give added emphasis:

But I warn you . . .

see **and**

can, may

Although frequently treated as interchangeable, <u>can</u> and <u>may</u> mean different things. <u>Can</u> is the present tense (past = 'could') and indicates capability:

I can play the piano.

It is, however, often used to seek or give permission:

Can I go now?

You can take over.

In formal usage, these should be *May I go now?* and *You may take over.*

It is important to avoid confusion with <u>may</u> when it means the same as 'might':

I may be late means *I might be late* and not *I have permission to be late.*

can't, cannot, can not

<u>Can't</u> is the shortened and less formal version of <u>cannot</u>. In written English, <u>cannot</u> would usually be preferable.

Can't seem, as in *I can't seem to get through to him*, is commonly used but is meaningless. You should avoid it.

<u>Cannot</u> can be ambiguous:

I cannot tell you how much I enjoyed your book means I am unable to find the words to express my admiration for your book, but *You cannot take too much trouble over your school work* means you must apply yourself totally to your school work.

Can not need to be two words when the not is emphasized:

You certainly can not have any more potatoes would, in more formal usage, be *You certainly may not . . .*

and in a sentence like:

Travel can not only give pleasure but also broadens the mind. Here the not belongs to 'not only . . . but also'.

case

Case is commonly used unnecessarily and as padding:

Is it the case that you lent him money? simply means *Did you lend him money?*

If that is the case . . . means 'If so . . .'

There are more single parents than was the case fifteen years ago is much better as *There are more single parents than there were fifteen years ago.*

Case is most appropriately used in a legal, medical or commercial context:

The magistrate ruled that there was no case to answer.

This is the worst case of indigestion I have treated.

In that case, I shall have to reconsider my offer.

Just in case used alone is very informal:

I will get another pint of milk just in case is, strictly, incomplete, even if the general meaning is understood. In more formal usage, the clause which completes the statement should be included:

I want you to wait at the station just in case his train is late.

character

Traditionally character refers to the special qualities of a person and, less frequently, of a place. It also refers to an individual in a play or novel.

52

Frequently now, <u>character</u> is used as a substitute for 'quality', 'kind', 'type', 'sort' and so on:

What was the character (= quality) *of his contribution to the discussion?*

. . . pamphlets of a revolutionary character (= kind).

The food was bland and without character (= taste).

. . . gardens of an unimaginative character (= type).

In contexts like these, it is better to be specific and say what you mean.

circumstances

Both <u>in the circumstances</u> and <u>under the circumstances</u> are used but in slightly different ways. The first is more general and simply recognizes a situation:

In the circumstances we had better leave things as they are.

The second has more force and draws attention to cause and effect:

He had been gagged and under the circumstances had difficulty attracting attention.

And use <u>under</u> when the statement is negative:

He refused to hand over the parcel under any circumstances (not *in any circumstances*).

Under no circumstances will I let you go.

compare to, compare with

Use <u>to</u> when comparing two elements which are unlike:

He compared her beauty to that of a rose in June.

Use <u>with</u> to draw attention to both similarities and differences:

Compared with the waiter, the manager was a model of courtesy.

<u>With</u> is always used in conjunction with *in comparison, by comparison* and *compared*, and when used intransitively:

His latest expedition cannot compare with his ascent of Everest.

53

compose, comprise, constitute

All three, in different ways, relate a whole to its parts. <u>Compose</u> and <u>constitute</u> refer to elements which together make up a whole or single unit. <u>Compose</u> is generally used in the passive form:

Steel is composed of iron and other elements.

These teams constitute the First Division.

<u>Comprise</u> means 'consists of', 'is made up of' and has the whole, not the parts, as the subject:

The orchard comprises apple, pear and damson trees.

<u>Comprised of</u> is always wrong.

data

Although <u>data</u> is a Latin plural (singular is 'datum'), meaning 'the facts given', it is frequently used with a singular verb:

Data to support his theory were very scarce is correct, but

There is not enough data to support his case is so widely used that the strictly correct form now seems pedantic.

days of the week

In written English, days of the week should always have a capital first letter and be written in full (Tuesday, Friday, etc.).

Use with preposition 'on': *I'll see you on Saturday.*

When the name of the day immediately follows 'next' or 'last' no preposition is needed:

I'll call for you next Monday.

The meeting was held last Wednesday.

description

<u>Description</u> should always be followed by 'of':

He gave us a detailed description of his family's hardships.

It should never be followed by 'about'.

despite, in spite of

These are interchangeable in straightforward statements:

Despite/in spite of his reluctance to go, he enjoyed the party.

Despite can sound old-fashioned; in spite of is more often used.

Despite of is wrong. 'But' should not be used with either:

But in spite of his protests, we went ahead is wrong.

different from, different than, different to

As we say that one thing 'differs from' another, different from is always acceptable:

His ideas are completely different from mine.

Different than is always wrong.

Different to, although commonly used, is avoided by careful users and is not recommended.

dilemma

Dilemma should not be used as just another word for 'problem' or 'difficulty'. It is correctly used when there is a choice of two, or possibly more, courses of action which are equally undesirable:

He faced the dilemma of handing back the stolen goods and being branded a thief or facing certain detection as he left the shop.

A dilemma which refers to attractive choices should only be used if irony is intended:

I can't choose between a slap-up meal and going to the party. What a dilemma!

disinterested, uninterested

These are often confused but mean completely different things. Disinterested means 'neutral', 'impartial', 'uninfluenced by personal considerations':

Every football match must have a disinterested referee.

Uninterested means 'bored', 'uninvolved', 'lacking enthusiasm':

He was completely uninterested in what we had to say.

double negatives

Obvious double negatives (*I haven't got no money. He wouldn't do nothing about it*), where the second negative cancels out the first, are easily avoided. Less easy to spot are semi-negative adverbs used with another negative word:

There were houses without hardly any windows should be *There were houses with hardly any windows.*

He couldn't barely stand the noise should be *He could hardly stand the noise.*

Sometimes 'not' with a negative is used as a stylistic device but, though effective in the right context, should be used sparingly:

It is not unlikely that he will show up is not quite the same as *He is likely to show up.*

In idiomatic or colloquial use, it is acceptable to write:

I shouldn't be surprised if it didn't rain before dark.

doubt

When it is a verb, doubt should be followed by 'that' in negative or interrogative contexts:

I do not doubt that he will return.

Do you now doubt that he caused the accident?

Otherwise, it is followed by 'if' or 'whether':

I doubt if the supports are strong enough.

I doubt whether we shall see such a storm again.

As a noun, doubt should be followed by 'about':

I have some serious doubts about the stability of the bridge.

Also in a negative statement:

I have no doubt about his being guilty this time.

<u>Doubt</u> should not be followed by 'but'.

downward, downwards

The first is an adjective which can also be adverbial:

He felt a downward rush of air.

After the storm, he had to revise downward his estimates.

<u>Downwards</u> is an adverb:

The slow spiral downwards into poverty.

due to, owing to, because of

All of these link elements of cause and effect, but they are used differently. <u>Because of</u> is the safest as it is always acceptable:

Because of the rain, we cancelled the picnic.

<u>Due to</u> and <u>owing to</u> are more specific and can trap the unwary. <u>Due</u> is an adjective and precedes the preposition <u>to</u> where the meaning is 'resulting from' or 'caused by'. It should be preceded by a noun and introduce a qualifying adjectival construction:

Loss due to recklessness on the Stock Market forced his resignation.

The beast's ferocity was due to its hunger.

<u>Owing to</u> is an adjective or a preposition:

We started early owing to the fine weather.

All trains will be delayed owing to a points failure.

If the result is conveyed by a finite verb, <u>owing to</u> should be used:

We were delayed owing to a landslide.

If the result is conveyed by a noun or a noun phrase, use <u>due to</u>:

The delay was due to a landslide.

Colloquially, <u>due to</u> is treated as a compound preposition and used to mean <u>because of</u> or 'caused by':

Due to atmospheric conditions, listeners and viewers in the Bristol area may have missed part of the News.

Ideally, this construction should not be used in formal writing.

each *see* **both**

each other, one another

Each other should be used when only two elements are involved:

Alice and William loved each other all their lives.

and when attention is being drawn to the elements individually:

They were bouncing each other up and down on the trampoline suggests an activity which is regulated and organized.

They were bouncing one another up and down . . . suggests something more haphazard where some, but not necessarily all, are taking part.

Use one another when more than two are referred to:

All the members of the club seemed to know one another well.

Although the distinction has been eroded, it is worth preserving.

e.g., i.e.

e.g. (an abbreviation of the Latin *exempli gratia*) means 'for example', 'for instance'. It is used before examples of what has already been mentioned:

Those who live far from railways and major roads, e.g. isolated cottagers, farmers and smallholders, will be given grants to help with transport and fuel costs.

i.e. (an abbreviation of the Latin *id est*) means 'that is' and is used before an explanation or another version of what has gone before:

St Valentine's Day, i.e. 14th February, falls on a Sunday this year.

In formal writing, 'for example' and 'that is to say' are preferable.

see **etc.**

either

Either is an adjective or a pronoun and means 'one or other of two'. It always requires a singular verb:

Either girl is qualified to captain the team.

Does either of your friends object to the proposal?

Where more than two elements are referred to, use 'any':

Do any of you want to join in?

Any of the team are willing to swim for charity.

either . . . or

Where both subjects are singular, use a singular verb:

Either Tom or Harry is the culprit.

If both subjects are plural, use a plural verb:

Either the Greeks or the Romans have already said it.

When one subject is singular and the other plural, the verb agrees with the subject nearer to it:

Either the accusers or the accused was not being truthful.

Either the accused or the accusers were not being truthful.

Generally, it is preferable to shape a sentence so that the plural subject is nearer the verb, which is then plural.

If singular subjects are in the form of pronouns and need different forms of the verb, the subject nearer the verb dictates the agreement:

Either I or he is going to fetch the bread.

Either he or I am going to fetch the bread.

Unavoidably, sentences like these are awkward. Rephrasing or using an invariable verb can solve the problem:

Either he is going to fetch the bread, or I am.

Either he or I (or I or he) will fetch the bread.

Either . . . or . . . or constructions should be avoided.

The <u>either . . . or</u> elements in a sentence should be balanced grammatically:

The examination was either easy or it was difficult needs amending for balance. It should be *The examination was either easy or difficult* or *Either the examination was easy or it was difficult.*

Take care over the position of <u>either</u> in a written sentence:

They must either retrace their steps or go on in the dark. Because 'they must' is part of the alternative suggested by <u>either</u>, those words need to come immediately after <u>either</u>. It should be *Either they must retrace their steps or* (*they must* is understood) *go on in the dark.*

elder, eldest/older, oldest

<u>Elder</u> and <u>eldest</u> are used only to refer to people, especially to indicate the order in which members of a family were born. <u>Elder</u> is used when comparing two people, as in *Tom's elder brother is James.* <u>Eldest</u> refers to more than two, as in *We have five grandchildren. The eldest has just gone to school.*

<u>Older</u> and <u>oldest</u> refer to the relative ages of people, animals and things. <u>Older</u> is used when comparing two, as in *Our house is much older than yours.* <u>Oldest</u> compares any numbers greater than two, as in *This is the oldest cow in the herd.*

<u>Older</u> can be followed by 'than'; <u>elder</u> cannot.

equal

Used as a verb, <u>equal</u> requires no preposition:

Two and two equal four.

Your time over 100 metres equals the previous record.

As an adjective, <u>equal</u> is followed by 'to' and means 'sufficiently able', 'adequate for the needs of':

He was not equal to carrying the whole load single-handed.

Referring to an element of competition, <u>equal</u> is followed by 'with':

He moved up to become equal with the others.

Usually, <u>more equal</u> and <u>most equal</u> should be avoided, but there are a few allowable exceptions:

When the money was divided out, our shares were more equal than we expected.

This was the most equal distribution of the money that we could have expected.

equally

Two or more things may be <u>equally</u> . . . followed by an adjective, but never by 'as':

Those two applications are equally as impressive is wrong and should be *Those two applications are equally impressive.*

All six candidates are equally qualified.

When <u>equally</u> compares two elements, they are joined by 'and', not 'or':

These shoes are equally suitable for town and (not *or*) *country wear.*

etc.

An abbreviation of the Latin *et cetera*, <u>etc.</u> means 'and so on', 'and so forth'. It is most appropriately used in business letters and technical documents. In more general forms of writing, 'and so on' or 'and so forth' are preferable. <u>Etc.</u> is usually preceded by a comma and followed by a full stop, and should only be used when a reasonable number of elements have been listed:

She sent us out to buy bread, butter, milk, fruit juice, etc. is acceptable but better as *She sent us . . . juice, and so on.*

Etc. should never be preceded by 'and' nor come at the end of a list introduced by e.g.

see **e.g.**

even

Even is an adverb which lends emphasis to a statement or a question. In formal writing, it should always be placed before the word it modifies or emphasizes:

Jacob watched the boxing match last week may be modified in several different ways. The position of *even* conveys the meaning:

Even Jacob watched the boxing match last week indicates that in addition to everyone else watching, Jacob watched the boxing match, or that, uncharacteristically, he watched it, that is, it was not something he would usually do.

Jacob even watched . . . week suggests that he watched the match in addition to everything else he did and implies that he had to make time to do it.

Jacob watched even . . . week suggests that he would have watched anything rather than nothing.

Jacob watched . . . even last week indicates that he watched the match as recently as last week and when we would not have expected him to.

ever

When it is emphasizing a statement, *ever* is a separate word:

What ever are we going to do?

Who ever made all this mess?

Why ever did you hide the key?

When *ever* is joined to another word, it generalizes a statement or a question:

Whatever we do, they won't be satisfied.

Whoever made this mess must clean it up.

Wherever you hide, they will find you.

However hard you try, you won't win.

Ever so followed by an adjective or an adverb is correct, but imprecise:

It is ever so kind of you to let us come is not suitable for formal writing and <u>ever so</u> on its own cannot modify a verb. *I enjoyed the Easter break ever so* should be avoided, so should <u>ever</u> on its own at the end of a phrase or sentence. *The smallest car ever* should be *The smallest car ever built.*

everybody, everyone
These words are interchangeable and refer to all the people included in a statement or a question. They are not used to refer to animals or things:
Everybody knows what you are thinking.
Everyone here is enjoying the party.
Although used to refer to a number greater than one, <u>everybody</u> and <u>everyone</u> are singular and take a singular verb. Where a personal pronoun or a possessive adjective appears, singular or plural should be used according to sense:
Everybody is doing their best.
Everyone is working his hardest.
Strict adherence to the rules can lead to awkwardness and clumsiness. 'They', 'them' and 'their' often now refer to single elements to avoid sentences like *Everybody is doing his or her best*; *Everyone is working one's hardest.*

every one
As two words, <u>every one</u> means 'each one singly, individually, separately' and is applied to people or things:
By the time the police arrived, every one of the vandals had disappeared.
Every one of the peaches was either bruised or bad.

except
<u>Except</u> excludes one or more elements from a larger category:

I have stamps from every European country except Denmark.

I have invited everyone except Charles and Dorothy.

except for

Generally, except for is colloquial and not used in formal contexts. There are, however, two forms of use which are acceptable. One is to begin a sentence:

Except for the two beggars moving in and out of the shadows, the square was deserted.

The other means 'if it were not for' and modifies the whole statement:

I would be on my feet again except for this persistent cough.

excepting

Excepting can be used instead of except when it follows 'not', 'always', 'without':

We are not excepting either of you from the cleaning rota.

Always excepting the danger of playing with matches, the children can do more or less what they like.

Without excepting even the children, the whole crowd were shut out of the school.

farther, farthest/further, furthest

As adjectives and adverbs, both forms are acceptable to indicate a measure of literal distance:

He has travelled much farther than we have.

That is the furthest we can travel in one day.

Some users prefer farther and farthest to indicate distance and use further only to mean 'more':

I cannot tell you anything further.

We shall have to look further into this matter.

Only further can be used as a verb:

He spent his life furthering his own business enterprises.

fewer, less

Both are used with plural nouns to express quantity, numbers and the countability of people and things. <u>Fewer</u> is used when referring to elements taken individually:

There were fewer than one hundred people in the audience.

I have fewer grey hairs than you.

Less is used when referring to quantity or mass:

He has less energy than he used to have.

I have less than £10 in my pocket.

The less you know the better.

We do not write <u>less</u> before 'price', 'number', etc. but refer to a *lower price* and a *smaller number*. We do, however, say *The number was less than expected* because we are comparing two numbers thought of as mathematical quantities. <u>Less</u> may be used correctly with a measurement number, as in *It cost less than 40p; Shoes can be repaired in less than three days; I have walked less than five miles today.*

first, firstly

Use both to number points in a list. Although the following forms are all acceptable:

Firstly . . . secondly . . . and thirdly . . .

First . . . secondly . . . and thirdly . . .

First . . . second . . . and third . . .

many writers prefer to avoid <u>firstly</u>. In the last example, <u>first</u> ('second' and 'third') are all adverbs which do not require a . . . ly ending.

Let's get this clear. First, I can't ride a horse; second, I don't own a horse, and third, I have no intention of buying a horse.

following

As a preposition, <u>following</u> should not be used as an alternative to 'after' or 'because of' as that leads to ambiguity:

The police detained the young woman following the carnival could mean that the police detained the young woman after the carnival, or that the young woman was detained while she was following the carnival. 'After' is the appropriate word here.

Following can, however, be used to mean 'after and as a result of':

Following a spate of accidents at this corner, traffic lights were installed.

As an adjective, following can mean 'next' (as in *the following day*) or 'about to be specified' (*You will need to bring the following equipment with you*).

for *see* **ago**

for ever, forever

Some writers treat these as interchangeable, but strictly, for ever means 'for all time', 'eternally':

Shakespeare will be honoured for ever in the annals of English literature.

Forever means 'continuously', 'incessantly':

Jack is forever lecturing us about the need to conserve natural resources.

If in doubt, for ever is preferable.

forward, forwards

Forward is both an adjective and an adverb and is always acceptable:

It is wise to do some forward planning.

We struggled to get the car to move forward.

Forwards is only an adverb. Although it is not obsolete, its use is much more limited:

The car moved forwards very slowly.

gentleman, lady

Traditionally, <u>gentleman</u> was a term which implied good breeding, courtesy and social status. It has mostly been replaced by 'man'. (Similarly, 'lady' has been replaced by 'woman'.) There are a few contexts where the older terms are still to be found. Public lavatories for men and women are labelled 'Gentlemen' and 'Ladies'; in spoken English, speech-makers' opening words are often, 'Ladies and Gentlemen'; as an exaggerated form of courtesy (*Would the gentleman in the third row please stand up?*; *I think this lady was before me*). But there is often a hint of irony:

You are an officer and a gentleman.

Gentlemen prefer blondes.

Ladies who lunch are seen at all the most fashionable restaurants.

get, got, gotten

<u>Get</u> and <u>Got</u> are inelegant words, common in informal usage, but inappropriate in formal written English:

I get all the blame is not wrong but is more elegantly expressed as *Everyone blames me*. *Have you got time to call in and see us?* is better as *Do you have time to call in and see us?*

Both may be used sparingly to give strength to a statement or question:

We get back at 4 o'clock.

I got through his novel in record time.

Careful writers will try to strike a balance between the natural and the stilted.

<u>Gotten</u> is an old variant of the past tense <u>got</u> and only appears in words like 'misbegotten' and phrases like 'ill-gotten gains'. Although fairly common in American English, it is not used in contemporary British English.

had rather *see* **would rather**

half

Half is a singular noun which requires a singular verb when it refers to quantity. (*Half of this cake is for you*), and a plural verb when it refers to a number (*Half of the players were penalized and sent off the field.*). Often, the word 'of' can be omitted: *Half the players . . . field.*

  see **fewer, less**

There is often uncertainty about whether or not half should be followed by a hyphen when it is joined to another word. The best approach is to refer to a dictionary, but a general rule is that a hyphen is needed when half and another word create a new compound which can be regarded as a single idea. These include 'half-timbered', 'half-hearted', 'half-term', 'half-pay', and so on. There is no hyphen in words and phrases such as 'halfway', 'halftone', 'half past two' and 'at half mast'.

hanged, hung

Hanged is used when someone has died by hanging:

  He hanged himself in his cell.

  Murderers used to be hanged publicly in England.

Otherwise, the past tense and past participle of 'hang' is hung:

  We hung the decorations in the hall.

  His portrait was hung in the National Gallery.

Hanged and hung in their literal meanings are unconnected with terms such as 'hanging around', 'hang-ups' and 'hanging loose', which are all recent slang.

hard, hardly

Hard is an adjective and an adverb. As an adverb, it is current in everyday use:

  Think hard about my offer.

The Inland Revenue comes down hard on people who evade tax.

Hardly is also an adverb, but of degree, which adds a strongly negative quality to a statement. You need no further negative:

I can (not *cannot*) *hardly hear you.* Here 'barely' or 'scarcely' would be acceptable alternatives.

Hardly can be followed by 'when', but not by 'than':

I had hardly arrived than he left is wrong and should be *I had hardly arrived when he left.*

'No sooner' used instead of hardly is followed by 'than', not 'when':

No sooner had I arrived than he started to argue again.

he, him, his/she, her, hers

These pronouns were used to specify gender where known. When a general, non gender-specific statement or question was written, he, him and his were used:

Every cyclist should have his brakes tested.

As this language came to be regarded as sexist, other forms of expression were needed:

Every cyclist should have his or her brakes tested is correct but clumsy.

Every cyclist should have their brakes tested is not strictly correct but is now acceptable.

see **everybody**, **everyone**

In formal writing, the best solution may be to phrase things differently:

All cyclists should have their brakes tested.

As cyclists, you should have your brakes tested.

This is a satisfactory solution only if the writer does not wish or need to begin a statement with 'each' or 'every'.

help

As a verb meaning 'avoid' or 'prevent oneself', help requires a present participle and should not be followed by 'but':

I couldn't help but laugh at her jokes sounds correct but is wrong. *I couldn't help laughing at her jokes* is simpler and more correct.

As a verb meaning 'assist', <u>help</u> can be followed by a direct object and/or an infinitive. Commonly in American English, it is also followed by 'to':

I offered to help them to get to New York would be *I offered to help them get to New York* in British English. Both are correct. A dictionary will offer guidance.

Where there is no direct object, omitting 'to' makes a statement or question stronger and terser:

This payment will help (to) save the company.

Will you help (to) tidy up?

hence, thence

Although an old-fashioned word meaning 'from here', <u>hence</u> is used in certain contexts. It lends a very formal, even stuffy, tone to what is written. It may be used by lawyers and academics to mean 'as a consequence', 'as a result' or 'from this time':

My client feels wronged; hence his plea of innocence.

Ten years hence the garden will be full of fruit.

With its original meaning, it would now only be found in works of literature:

Get thee hence. Return not till the deed is done.

<u>Thence</u> meaning 'from there' is used in much the same way. 'From <u>hence</u>' and 'from <u>thence</u>' are always wrong. 'Henceforward' and 'henceforth', both meaning 'from now on', may be found but are not often appropriate.

historic, historical

Although some regard these as interchangeable, they mean different things.

70

Historic is correctly used to describe a past event which may or may not have seemed important at the time but which is now regarded as of major significance:

Their historic meeting led many years later to the setting up of the European Common Market.

People have questioned the historic decision to televise Parliament.

Historical refers to the study of history and to past events in general:

You have to look at social progress with an historical perspective.

All the historical documents relating to the slave trade can be made available.

hopefully

Hopefully is an adverb which means 'with hope', 'in a hopeful mood'. It is also now commonly used to mean 'we hope', 'it is to be hoped', etc. This second form is widely accepted but needs to be used carefully to avoid ambiguity.

The shoppers waited hopefully for the doors to open is unambiguous.

Hopefully, we will be there by 7.30 is not popular with purists but is also quite clear.

Misunderstanding may result if hopefully is placed immediately before the verb:

The team will hopefully meet us in Berlin may mean that we hope the team will meet us in Berlin, or that the team will meet us in Berlin full of a spirit of hope.

In formal contexts, hopefully (and other words such as 'frankly', 'mercifully' and 'thankfully') should not be used to modify the meaning of a whole sentence.

see **sentence adverbs**

how ever, however

As two words, how ever lends emphasis to a statement and is an interrogative adverb in a question:

How ever you put it, that suggestion is going to give offence.

How ever did you know where we were?

As one word, however expresses a general, unemphatic idea, or it may simply mean 'but', 'nevertheless', 'yet':

However he divides his money, some people are going to be disappointed.

We don't expect to see her, however, as she is going by sea.

When however means 'but', both words should not appear in the same sentence, except when however is used as it is in the first example above:

But, however he divides . . . disappointed.

Unlike 'but', however can appear in different positions in a sentence (it is better to avoid the beginning and the end), and its position affects the meaning:

The director, however, did not like the tone of the working party's report means that the director did not like the report but, it can be assumed, everybody else did.

The director disliked, however, the tone of the working party's report suggests that the director was happy with the content of the report but not its tone.

I, me/we, us

I is a singular nominative pronoun subject and is always written with a capital letter. Me is a singular accusative pronoun object. When either appears alone in a sentence, there is no difficulty:

Jill and I are going for a walk.

Will you take me with you?

When I and me appear in the same sentence, some people are not sure which to use:

They brought some coffee for my sister and I is what many people would consider correct. But it is wrong. If the elements are looked at separately, nobody would write *They brought some coffee for . . . I*. There is a belief that I is more refined than me, but that doesn't alter the fact that it is wrong. It can work the other way round:

My sisters, my cousins, my aunts and me will be at the wedding is wrong. Again, if the elements are broken down, it is clear that there is something seriously wrong with . . . *me will be at the wedding*.

Although in speech, most of us would say, *It is me*, in writing, the correct form, *It is I*, should be used.

We and us are the plural forms and the same rules apply, as they do to 'they' and 'them'.

see **myself**

i.e. *see* **e.g.**

if

For a small word, if can cause a lot of trouble when it is used, as it often is, to replace 'though' or 'whether'. When if is used instead of 'though':

The rock climb, if dangerous, is great fun could mean that the climb is fun even though it is dangerous, or that it is only fun if it is dangerous. This should be *The rock climb, though dangerous, is great fun* if that is what is intended.

When if is used instead of 'whether':

Please let me know if you are taking the exam might mean that I do not want to know if you are not taking the exam, or I only want you to tell me if you are taking the exam. To avoid ambiguity, it should be *Please let me know whether or not you are taking the exam*.

When if introduces a clause which suggests a realistic, likely or possible condition, use the ordinary indicative form of the verb:

If he is coming on the 10.35 train, ask him in for coffee.

When <u>if</u> introduces an uncertain or hypothetical condition, use the subjunctive form of the verb:

If he were to arrive first, we should take the chance to speak to him alone.

see **subjunctive**

Some people like to use <u>if</u> combined with 'when'. Both are rarely needed as they serve the same purpose:

I will write if and when I have time is wrong. Omit either 'and when' or 'if and' to be correct.

imply, infer

These are frequently confused but they mean completely different things. <u>Imply</u> means to 'suggest' or 'hint' indirectly rather than to state unequivocally:

The boss implied that anyone taking strike action would be sacked means that anyone taking strike action might be sacked, not that they definitely would be.

<u>Infer</u> means to 'deduce' or 'draw a conclusion' from available evidence:

The workforce inferred from the boss's statement that their jobs were at risk.

The most common mistake is the use of <u>imply</u> in place of <u>infer</u>.

in spite of *see* despite

in to, into

These are different; do not confuse them. <u>In to</u> combines two words each in a separate role. <u>In</u> is an adverb which is followed by the preposition <u>to</u>, or <u>to</u> is part of the infinitive:

The waiter took coffee in to them.

He came in to tell us it was time to go.

<u>Into</u> is a preposition:

74

The waiter took coffee into the dining room.

As prepositions, <u>in</u> and <u>into</u> are sometimes interchangeable:

She put the notes in/into her purse.

<u>Into</u> tends to suggest the physical movement of someone or something from outside to inside. <u>In</u> suggests enclosure. There are occasions when <u>in</u> and <u>into</u> cannot be interchanged without loss of meaning:

She waited in the lobby for half an hour before going into the meeting.

involve

This is a vogue word which originally meant 'enfold', 'enwrap', 'envelop' or 'surround' and giving an indication of close association or linkage, intentness, deep thought, engrossment or entanglement:

He was closely involved in planning the invasion.

Beware of getting involved with the criminal fraternity.

<u>Involved</u> can also be correctly used to mean 'complicated', 'complex', 'tortuous', etc.:

His involved explanation of the cause of the war left us baffled.

<u>Involved</u> is frequently used in an imprecise way when it is unhelpful and often unnecessary. A better word can always be found:

Some alterations to the barn will be involved (should be needed).

Ten carpenters will be involved (should be employed) in this job.

Rebuilding the barn will involve (should be entail) a large cash outlay.

Their lack of involvement (should be interest or commitment) was criticized.

I will not be involved in (should be drawn into) the argument.

The money involved will take years to collect. (Involved can be omitted altogether.)

. . . ise, . . . ize

In many cases, both are acceptable. The . . . ize ending is tending to replace the more traditional . . . ise and has always been more popular in American English. There are some words, however, which must always end . . . ise. They are:

advertise   advise   apprise   arise   chastise   circumcise
comprise   compromise   demise   despise   devise
disguise   emprise   enfranchise   enterprise   excise
improvise   incise   merchandise   premise   prise (to force)
promise   revise   supervise   surmise   surprise   televise.

its, it's

These are frequently confused and mean completely different things. Its is a possessive pronoun (like 'your', 'his', 'our', etc.) and never has an apostrophe between the t and the s:

Give the dog its bone.

The eagle circled over its territory.

It's is a shortened version of 'it is' or 'it has' and needs the apostrophe to indicate that letters are missing:

It's a beautiful day.

It's been a great pleasure to meet you.

just

As an adjective, just means 'fair', 'equitable' and presents no difficulties. As an adverb, it means 'precisely', 'only', 'exactly', 'at this moment', 'very recently':

It is just eight o'clock (= 'precisely', 'exactly'). *It is just exactly eight o'clock* is wrong. Just or 'exactly' would be correct; the sentence does not need both.

Kate arrived just a few moments ago (= 'only').

Joe is at the theatre just now (= 'at this moment').

When <u>just</u> means 'very recently', it requires the perfect tense of the verb:

The Queen has just returned to the Palace.

When <u>just</u> is used to mean 'simply' or 'only', its position in a sentence affects the meaning:

I am just not interested.

I am not just interested, I need to know.

The brakes are just holding means that the brakes are holding with some difficulty.

Just the brakes are holding means only the brakes are holding; there are no other restraints.

Beware of <u>just</u> used as padding:

I just love you.

He's just the best.

kind of, sort of, type of

It is important to avoid introducing sloppy speech habits when writing clear English. In the singular, <u>kind of</u> and <u>sort of</u> should usually be preceded by 'this' or 'that' and followed by a singular noun and verb:

This kind of bicycle is a mountain bike.

Making that sort of pudding will test your skills.

This type of house is difficult to heat.

In a question, putting 'a' before the noun changes the meaning:

What kind of bicycle is this? asks what make or classification it is. *It's a mountain bike.*

What kind of a bicycle is this? asks about its qualities and performance. *It's designed for racing over rough terrain.*

In the plural form, <u>kinds of</u>, <u>sorts of</u> and <u>types of</u> refer to a singular noun but require a plural verb:

These kinds of bicycle are built for racing.

These sorts of dishes are very high in calories.

These types of houses are difficult to heat.

In such cases, a preferable form would be:

This kind of bicycle is built for racing; this sort of dish is high in calories; this type of house is difficult to heat, where all parts are kept singular.

An alternative would be *Bicycles of this kind are . . .; Dishes of this sort are . . .; Houses of this type are . . .,* where the plural verb ('are') agrees with the plural noun in each case.

If it is the <u>kind</u>, <u>sort</u> or <u>type</u> which is plural, the following noun is singular, but the verb is plural:

Four of these kinds of bicycle are built for racing.

Some of these sorts of dish are high in calories.

I like both these types of house.

Used adverbially, <u>kind of</u> and <u>sort of</u> are too informal for written English:

She is kind of programmed to respect everyone she works with.

He sort of lands on his feet every time.

In the plural form, however, they may be acceptable in all but the most formal contexts:

She has had all kinds of problems with her children.

He got into all sorts of trouble at school.

lady *see* **gentleman**

last

When used as an adjective, <u>last</u> requires care as it could mean 'the final' element in a sequence:

The last person to leave puts out the lights.

or, it could mean 'the most recent':

The last time we met, I promised to give you this book.

Misunderstandings can arise:

The climax was reached in the last chapter could refer to the preceding chapter or to the final chapter in the book. It is preferable to find an alternative way of expressing the same thing:

The climax was reached in the preceding/final chapter (depending upon which is intended).

<u>Last</u> presents no difficulty when the context makes the meaning clear:

I saw the last five minutes of the programme.

Joe was at the concert last night.

He was the last to enter the room.

lay, lie

Confusion between these words is common. <u>Lay</u> means to place something on a horizontal surface or put something carefully in a particular position. It is a transitive verb and takes a direct object. Its principal parts are <u>lay</u>, <u>laying</u>, <u>laid</u>, <u>have laid</u>:

Will you lay the cloth on the table?

They are laying gas pipes under the road.

He laid sheets of cardboard on the floor.

We have laid our cards on the table.

<u>Lie</u> means to be or to remain in a horizontal or supine position. It is an intransitive verb and so has no direct object. Its principal parts are <u>lie</u>, <u>lying</u>, <u>lay</u>, <u>have lain</u>:

I always lie in bed until 7.30.

He is lying in bed with a bad cold.

I lay in the sun for far too long.

They have lain awake all night.

The confusion between <u>lay</u> and <u>lie</u> may be due to the fact that the present tense of <u>lay</u> and the past tense of <u>lie</u> are the same word.

79

Lay meaning 'produce eggs' does not require its direct object as it has a particular meaning and the object ('eggs') is understood:

Do these old hens still lay?

Lie meaning 'tell falsehoods', 'be untruthful' presents no difficulty. Its forms are regular, lie, lying, lied, have lied, and the context makes the meaning clear.

less *see* fewer

like

Used as a preposition, like is followed by the object form (the accusative) of pronouns ('me', 'them', etc.), or a noun or noun equivalent:

Take a girl like me. (Take a girl like I is wrong.)

It is not like them (not they) to be late.

He can swim like a fish.

It is a common mistake to use like instead of 'as', 'as if' or 'as though':

Cook the steaks like you did yesterday is wrong and should be *Cook the steaks as you did yesterday.*

He talked like he didn't realize he was being overheard should be *He talked as if/as though he . . . overheard.*

Meaning can and may be altered by replacing like with 'as':

Of course, like an artist, I advise the Impressionists. 'But I am not an artist' is understood.

Of course, as an artist, I advise the Impressionists. 'And I am an artist' is understood.

many, much

Many refers to large, countable numbers and requires a plural verb:

Many hands make light work.

80

Many holiday resorts are deserted in winter.

There are not many people here today.

<u>Much</u> refers to a large, uncountable quantity and requires a singular verb:

There is not much coal left.

In negative statements and in questions, both <u>many</u> and <u>much</u> may be used as appropriate.

In positive statements, <u>much</u> is often correct, but does tend to sound rather formal:

He gave much thought to what he was going to say might, less formally, be, *He gave a lot of thought to what he was going to say.*

<u>Many</u> can also replace 'a lot of' or 'lots of' to make a sentence more formal:

There are lots of fish in this river./There are many fish in this river.

If 'a great' is used before <u>many</u>, it can give added emphasis:

There are a great many fish in this river.

Some writers prefer to avoid this construction and would use instead, *There is a large number of fish in this river.*

<u>Much</u> can be used to modify participles (e.g. *He has been much criticized. Your advice is much sought after*) where 'very' would be used to modify an adjective (e.g. *He is very wise. You are not being very decisive*).

Some participles having lost their verbal character, point and vigour through regular use, are treated like adjectives and require 'very' before them (*I am very willing to help. She is very self-possessed*).

may, might

Care is needed in the choice of tense of this auxiliary verb so that meaning is clear.

The present tense *may* and the past tense <u>might</u> are used to convey permission, possibility or probability:

May I rest in the shade?

She asked whether she might rest in the shade.

He may retire early.

I think he might retire early.

The first example requests permission. It could read *Might I rest in the shade?* but that introduces an element of hesitation or reserve in seeking permission.

In the last example, <u>might</u> suggests a stronger element of doubt than <u>may</u> does in the example before it. Either would be acceptable, but the meaning is subtly different.

<u>May</u> or <u>might</u> can be used in the perfect tense to record a past event:

Lucy may have done it. Lucy might have done it. Again, the meaning is slightly different:

. . . may have . . . suggests a possibility which still exists and is unresolved.

. . . might have . . . suggests a possibility that no longer exists.

Lucy may have arrived today, but I shan't know until I telephone tonight.

Lucy might have arrived today; but her car broke down on the motorway.

<u>May</u> and <u>might</u> are both used to suggest possibilities now and in the future. <u>May</u> is used to refer to a genuinely likely possibility:

With black clouds gathering, it looks as if it may rain before dark.

<u>Might</u> is used when the possibility is less likely or very slight:

Next year I might win the lottery and stop work for ever.

see **can, may**

me *see* **I**

might *see* **may**

much *see* **many**

myself

Recently <u>myself</u>, as an emphatic personal pronoun, has been moving into the language as a substitute for 'I' or 'me':

My husband and myself enjoyed the display is false and ludicrous. As is:

Please call anyone in the Sales Department or myself for further information. If the elements are separated out (. . . *myself enjoyed the display*; *Please call . . . or myself . . .*), it becomes clear how absurd these usages are.

Myself is used correctly as a reflexive, emphatic pronoun:

After the accident, I could not feed myself without help.

I towelled myself down after my swim in the sea.

Other forms such as 'himself', 'herself', 'oneself' can be more stylish and pleasing than the simple 'him', 'her' and 'one':

Her winning entry – a snap of mother, father and herself – was framed and presented to her.

The rapport between one's team and oneself is very important.

see **I, me**

nature

Unless referring to the natural world (e.g. *nature red in tooth and claw*), <u>nature</u> is an overused and vague word favoured by prolix and pompous writers:

A remark of that nature was unnecessary should be *That was an unnecessary remark.*

What is the nature of your quarrel? should be *What is your quarrel about?*

Saving is in the nature of an investment in the future is much better as *Saving is an investment.*

neither

As an adjective or a pronoun, <u>neither</u> refers to only two elements, never more, and requires a singular verb:

Neither captain has lost a game this season.

There are two umbrellas but neither is mine.

Where there are more than two elements, 'no', 'none' or 'not' should be used:

No public clock told the correct time.

None of the clocks was accurate.

Not one of the clocks was accurate.

When <u>neither</u> is joined with 'nor', singular elements require a singular verb, and plural elements a plural verb:

Neither Martin nor Jonathan owns a yacht.

Neither the lettuces nor the radishes were fresh.

If one item is singular and the other plural, the verb agrees with the element nearer to it:

Neither the drinks nor the food was satisfactory.

Neither the food nor the drinks were satisfactory.

If both items are singular but include a pronoun which requires its own verb form (e.g. 'I have', 'she has', etc.), the verb agrees with the item nearer to it:

Neither my brother nor I have the right to be here.

Neither you nor she has the right to be here.

Alternative, parallel ideas should be expressed with grammatical balance:

He had neither the strength nor was his mind sharp enough for the job is unbalanced (a noun is followed by a whole clause).

He had neither the strength nor the intelligence for the job is balanced (a noun is followed by another noun).

non-

This negative prefix often creates a more restrained and less emphatic opposite than 'un-', 'im-', 'in-', etc.

'Unprofessional' describes a person or conduct which does not match up to professional status; <u>non</u>-professional suggests amateur status and implies no blame. 'Insensitive' suggests a lack of finer feelings; <u>non</u>-sensitive describes imperviousness and, again, implies no accusation. Although useful, this construction should not be over-used.

none

As a pronoun, <u>none</u> should be followed by a singular or plural verb according to the context. Where <u>none</u> clearly means 'no one' or 'not one', the verb is singular:

None would believe a word he said.

None of the children wants to go to school.

The verb is also singular when <u>none</u> alludes to an amount or a quantity:

None of her time was ever wasted.

When <u>none</u> means 'not any' or 'no people', the plural verb is needed:

There are none present so foolish as to believe him.

None have survived to tell the story.

not only . . . but (also)

As with 'neither . . . nor' (*see* **neither**), the use of singular or plural verbs is dictated by the content of a statement, and writers should aim for symmetry. Sometimes <u>also</u> can be omitted:

He not only lost the election but (also) forfeited his deposit. Alternatively, this could be *He not only . . . but forfeited his deposit as well.*

> *Not only were the fish ignoring the bait, but the stream was now flowing too fast.*

not un . . . *see* **double negatives**

no use *see* **use**

numbers

Figures (not words) should be used for ages (*He was 6*), dates (*14 July* or *14th July*), money (*20 pence*), heat (*75 degrees*), scores (*3–2, 2 sets to 1*), time (*10 minutes, 8 o'clock*), distance (*3 feet, 80 kilometres*), votes (*He received 17,450 votes*), weights (*5 grammes, 50 tonnes*), volume (*14 cubic metres*) and area (*100 hectares*).

Words (not figures) should be used at the beginning of sentences (*Five years ago . . .*), for indefinite amounts (*There were hundreds of spectators*) and certain street names (*Fifth Avenue* but *East 89th Street*). Contracts and other legal documents tend to show figures followed (as confirmation) by the same amount in words, as £100 (one hundred pounds only).

Generally, numbers should be written as figures wherever possible. There are conventions rather than rules – some writers choose to express numbers from one to ten in words, and in figures from 11 onwards, but there is no obvious reason for doing this.

Whatever the writer's choice, it is important to be consistent and to avoid sentences like *There were six girls and 5 boys*.

off

As a preposition, <u>off</u> should never be followed by 'of':

He dived off (not *off of*) *the rock*.

Nor should it replace 'from':

I bought it from (not *off*) *the junk dealer in the market*.

older, oldest *see* **elder, eldest**

one

This generalizing pronoun can easily be over-used, when it sounds ridiculous. It should not be used as a falsely modest substitute for 'I' or 'we':

One is pleased with the thought of having been of some service in environmental issues.

For consistency, <u>one</u> is followed by <u>one</u>, 'one's', 'oneself', and this can lead to artificial and overwrought constructions:

When one receives one's exam results, one may hesitate to open the envelope for fear of one's not having done justice to oneself or one's teachers.

It is always advisable to try to construct an acceptable variation:

When you receive your exam results, you may hesitate to open the envelope for fear of your not having done justice to yourself or your teachers.

Other preferable forms are 'we', 'they', 'people', 'anyone', 'someone', 'a person', etc.

When <u>one</u> refers to a particular person (rather than the whole human race), it should be followed by 'he', 'she', 'his', 'her', etc. as appropriate:

The two friends decided to buy a swimsuit each; one chose blue, her favourite colour, the other chose black.

one another *see* **each other**

only

Place this adverb as near as possible to the word it modifies. As a general rule, <u>only</u> modifies what immediately follows it. If nothing follows it, it modifies what immediately precedes it. Meaning is determined by the position of <u>only</u> in a sentence:

The racehorses are grazing in the southern enclosure.

Only the racehorses . . . enclosure means that no others are.

The only racehorses . . . enclosure means that there are no other racehorses.

The racehorses only . . . enclosure is unclear and not idiomatic.

The racehorses are only grazing . . . enclosure means they are not doing anything else but grazing.

The racehorses . . . only in the southern enclosure means they are not grazing anywhere but the southern enclosure.

The racehorses . . . in the only southern enclosure means that this is the only enclosure in the south.

The racehorses . . . in the southern only enclosure could mean that the southern enclosure is the only fenced area, but it is unclear.

The racehorses . . . southern enclosure only means the horses are not grazing anywhere else.

When there is no danger of misunderstanding or ambiguity, <u>only</u> should be put between the subject and the main verb according to idiom:

I have only written three postcards this morning.

<u>Only</u> should not be used as a conjunction meaning 'but' or 'however':

A picnic on the beach would be a treat only I can't spare the time is wrong.

on to, onto
When used as a preposition, either is acceptable:

He jumped on to/onto the bus as it was moving off.

Two words are needed when <u>on</u> as an adverb is followed by <u>to</u> as a preposition or indicating the infinitive:

He went on to the next station by mistake.

Take this path, then keep straight on to reach the river.

see **in to, into**

or
<u>Or</u> indicates choice between two or more elements. If they are singular, use a singular verb:

Possibly John or Fred knows where it has been hidden.

If the elements are plural, use a plural verb:

Ice creams or drinks are not to be consumed on these premises.

If one element is singular and the other plural, the verb agrees with the one nearer to it:

Two half-litre cartons or a litre one is what we need.

When or offers choice including pronouns, the form is determined by the nearer pronoun:

You or he is responsible for the damage.

He or you are responsible for the damage.

Are you or your wife representing us at the wedding?

These usages can appear clumsy in written English and it may be better to phrase things differently:

You are or he is responsible for the damage.

One of you is responsible for the damage.

Are you or is your wife representing us at the wedding?

It is acceptable to start a sentence with or which should be followed by a comma:

Or, so I am told.

other than

This should be used adjectivally, not as an adverb. It is usually found in negative contexts:

There was no sound other than the wind in the willows.

The stranger was none other than King Richard in disguise.

At no time was his performance as Othello other than brilliant.

Other should not be combined with 'but' or 'except', though either may replace other than:

He had no money other than large notes can be *He had no money but large notes.*

Every other buttonhole than yours was a rose can be *Every buttonhole except yours was a rose.*

otherwise

As an adverb, otherwise means 'in every way except this':

Robert has no respect for spelling, otherwise he writes very well.

I cannot speak about the close of the meeting otherwise than briefly.

When <u>otherwise</u> means 'or else', it is unnecessary to include 'or':

Press the putty in carefully, otherwise (not *or otherwise*) *you may break the glass.*

Some writers use <u>otherwise</u> as an adjective or a pronoun:

We shall move the jigsaw, completed or otherwise, from the table.

The whole class, culprits and otherwise, had to stay behind.

Purists prefer:

We shall move the jigsaw, completed or not, from the table.

The whole class, culprits and others, had to stay behind.

ought

As an old past tense of 'owe' (which is now only used in the present and is always followed by the infinitive verb), <u>ought</u> cannot be used with an auxiliary verb:

I ought to pay the milkman and *Ought I to pay the milkman?* are correct.

Had I ought to pay the milkman? is wrong.

You ought not (or *oughtn't*) *to drink so much* is correct.

You didn't (or *hadn't*) *ought to drink so much* is wrong.

Occasionally <u>ought</u> may be replaced by 'should' when it expresses expectation, duty, obligation, etc.:

These plums should be ready for picking tomorrow expresses expectation and anticipation.

You should visit your family more often implies duty and obligation.

<u>Ought</u> is much stronger than 'should' and is used to express greater expectation or obligation:

You ought to visit your family more often is a much stronger statement than *You should . . . . often.*

A friend might say, *You should lose weight.* A doctor might say, *You ought to lose weight.*

owing to *see* **due to**

perfect

As an adjective, <u>perfect</u> describes an absolute state, indicating that something is as good as it can possibly be. <u>Perfect</u>, therefore, should not be preceded by 'more' or 'most'. It is, however, acceptable to use 'nearly <u>perfect</u>' and 'almost <u>perfect</u>', which expresses a state of approaching (but not assuming) perfection:

The weather was nearly perfect for our outing.

She skated in an almost perfect circle.

see **absolute adjectives**

preface

As a verb, <u>preface</u> requires 'with' before a noun:

He prefaced his address with a word or two of welcome.

'by' before the gerund:

He prefaced his sermon by referring to the earthquake.

or 'by' after a passive voice even if a noun follows:

His sermon was prefaced by a reference to the earthquake.

prefer

When <u>prefer</u> expresses a comparison between elements, it is followed by 'to':

I prefer golf to bowls.

Amanda prefers dining at The Blue Boar to The Black Dog.

When <u>prefer</u> comes before an infinitive, some rearrangement is required:

Marion prefers to swim to to play tennis and *Marion prefers to swim to play tennis* are both wrong, and should be:

Marion prefers swimming to playing tennis or *Marion prefers to swim rather than to play tennis. (Marion prefers to swim than to play tennis* is wrong.)

provided, providing

<u>Provided</u>, with or without 'that' (both are acceptable), should be used, rather than <u>providing</u>. The term indicates that a prior condition has to be met:

Rupert plans to go bird-watching provided (that) his binoculars are repaired in time.

On most occasions, 'if' would be a preferred substitute for <u>provided (that)</u>.

question *see* beg the question

rather

<u>Rather</u> is an overworked and often meaningless word. It should not be used as padding:

I find that little gadget you gave me rather handy. (<u>Rather</u> should be omitted.)

<u>Rather</u> may legitimately be used to tone down, mitigate or make ironic statements and questions:

I find it rather unmannerly of you to walk into my office without knocking.

<u>Rather</u> softens but does not remove the criticism. Without <u>rather</u>, the criticism would be more final and abrupt.

When used for emphasis, the position of <u>rather</u> in a sentence is important:

I rather suspect that we should be making a mistake to appoint you.

<u>Rather</u> here appears to exonerate the rest of the interviewing panel.

I suspect that we should be making rather a mistake to appoint you.

In this case, the implication is that the interviewers are agreed and attention is focused on the mistake.

<u>Rather</u> can be an alternative for 'very':

He makes a rather delicious plum pudding.

That outfit is rather smart.

That was a rather stupid question.

<u>Rather</u> can serve to correct or qualify something just stated, or to introduce more detail:

I was shaving, or rather just about to start, when the telephone rang.

I was approached by a beggar, or rather by someone who looked like a beggar but turned out to be someone I knew.

When <u>rather</u> is combined with 'than', it expresses a comparison:

This home-made beer has turned out rather better than I expected.

<u>Rather than</u> cannot replace 'than' on its own after a comparative:

He was more concerned with the enjoyment of food than (not *rather than*) *his need to lose weight.*

see **would rather**

reason

Because <u>reason</u> already incorporates the notions of 'because', 'owing to', 'for', etc., it is a tautology to write '*the reason why*', '*the reason is because*', and so on.

Many writers avoid '*The reason why . . .*'. In place of *The reason why she emigrated was . . .*, they prefer:

The reason that she emigrated was . . .; *The reason she emigrated was . . .* or *Her reason for emigrating was . . .*

<u>Reason</u> should not be followed by 'because' later in the same sentence:

The reason for the delay is because the umpire has not arrived is wrong and should be:

The reason for the delay is that the umpire has not arrived; or The match was delayed because the umpire had not arrived.

shall, will

The traditional rule, when expressing future time, is to use <u>shall</u> after the first person singular and plural:

I shall arrive between 6 and 6.30.

We shall be there to meet you.

and <u>will</u> after everything else:

You will/they will/it will/Uncle Jack will . . .

However, to express resolve, intention, determination, commands, etc., this pattern is reversed:

I/we will go despite the weather.

You shall be successful in the end.

It shall be done.

Uncle Jack shall get better.

<u>Will</u> is now very widely used instead of <u>shall</u> and is acceptable. It is appropriate in questions like:

You won't let me down, will you? (Won't is an abbreviation of 'will not'.)

Will you have tea or coffee?

Won't you come in out of the cold?

<u>Shall</u> should be used in questions like:

Shall we go fishing now or later?

Let's sail round the island tomorrow, shall we?

Where shall I get a meal at this time of night?

Shall I bring you a copy of today's paper?

she *see* he

should, would

To present a future event from a point in the past, <u>should</u> is used with 'I' and 'we' and <u>would</u> is used with everything else.

94

We said we should continue playing until 6 o'clock.

You said you would be here before dark.

Increasingly, <u>would</u> is supplanting <u>should</u> with first person singulars and plurals. <u>Should</u> is used when 'ought to' is intended:

We should get together more often.

You should go and see that film.

<u>Would</u> is used when it means 'used to':

She would write to her son every week.

I would go on holiday at the same time every year.

Abbreviations such as 'I'd' (*I should* or *I would*), 'you'd', 'they'd', etc. are widely used but are best avoided in formal writing.

since *see* **ago**

slow, slowly

In all formal contexts, <u>slow</u> is an adjective and <u>slowly</u> an adverb:

Heavy vehicles should stay in the slow lane.

He walks so slowly that everyone else loses patience.

Comparative forms are 'slower' and 'slowest'.

There are a number of idiomatic expressions which are acceptable in context:

The workforce threatened a go-slow in their wage dispute.

My journey took twice as long because of trains running slow.

so

Both <u>so</u> and <u>so that</u> are used to introduce a purpose clause:

She went to the library every day so (that) she could read the new magazines.

Although <u>so that</u> is always correct, and <u>so</u> on its own is less formal, a simpler construction is often available and preferable:

She went to the library every day to read the new magazines.

So that tends to add weight to a statement which may not be intended:

So that there should be absolutely no doubt about our destination, we covered our luggage with address labels.

So alone can be used to introduce a clause which conveys a result:

Rabbits had eaten all the lettuces so we had no salad for the picnic.

So with 'as to' and the infinitive conveys purpose. It is a formal and dated construction and a simpler form can usually be found:

She climbed the mountain so as to reach the top would be better as *She climbed the mountain to reach the top* (omitting 'so as').

It may be used to lend emphasis where that is intended:

So as to make it quite clear who is in charge, I want everyone to address me as 'Sir'.

So preceded by 'do' can take the place of a word or phrase previously used to avoid repetition:

If you want to rest for half an hour, by all means do so.

He said I could take any painting I fancied and I did so.

The bus should have stopped but failed to do so.

Is Mary at home? I don't think so refers to the whole question and it doesn't have to be repeated.

sort of *see* **kind of**

spelling
It is always worth checking to ensure spelling is correct. A computer spellcheck program may not be reliable; a dictionary always should be. Some commonly misspelled words include the following:

abattoir
abbreviate
accessible
accidentally
accommodate
achievement
acknowledgment
address
adjacent
adolescence
advice (noun)
advise (verb)
aggravate
aging
alcohol
allege
all right
alright
all ready
already
all together
altogether
analysis
apparent
appearance
argument
assassinate
attendance
beggar
believe
bourgeois
bulletin

> USE THE BLANK SPACES FOR WRITING DOWN ANY OTHER WORDS THAT YOU OFTEN FIND DIFFICULT TO SPELL CORRECTLY.

bureau
bureaucracy
business
calendar
category
ceiling
changeable
chic
chief
choose
coeducational
coefficient
collectable
commit
committee
comparative
competent
complement
compliment
confer
conscience
conscious
consistent
controlled
controversy
convener
coolly
correspondent
counterfeit
criticism
criticize
crux

curiosity
damageable
deceive
decimate
decision
decrepit
defendant
definite
deposit
dependable
description
desiccate
desirable
despair
desperate
develop
development
disabuse
disappear
disappoint
disastrous
disrobe
divide
divine
dormitory
ecstasy
embarrass
environment
equatable
equip
equivalent
especially

essence
exaggerate
exceed
excellent
excess
exhilarate
existence
experience
explain
explanation
façade
familiar
fascinate
fiendish
fiery
firsthand
first-rate
flammable
flotation
forceful
forcible
foreign
friend
fulfil
gaiety
gauge
goddess
government
grammar
grievance
grizzly
guarantee

guttural
habitat
handiwork
harass
headachy
height
heroes
homogeneous
homogenous
hoping
horizontal
humankind
humorous
hydrogen
hypocrisy
iceberg
idiosyncrasy
imagery
imagination
immanent
immediately
imminent
impel
incidentally
incur
independence
independent
indispensable
inimical
inquire
inquiry
insistence

intelligent
interrupt
inventor
irrelevant
irreverent
jelly baby
jellyfish
jodhpurs
judgment
juggernaut
kayak
kernel
kilogram
kilometre
knowledgeable
lawsuit
leisure
license
lifelong
lifetime
lollipop
loneliness
longevity
loose
lose
lumbar
manoeuvre
marriage
matey
mathematics
media
medicine

medieval
millennium
miniskirt
mischievous
misogyny
mortgage
Muslim
naive
necessary
necessity
newspaper
niece
noncommittal
nonsuit
normalize
nosy
noticeable
obsolescent
occasion
occasionally
occur
occurrence
omission
omit
omitted
oneness
original
outdated
overdevelop
over-use
parallel
passable

pastime
persuade
playwright
portrayal
practice (noun)
practise (verb)
precede
prejudice
presumptuous
prevalence
principal
principle
privilege
procedure
prodigy
professional
prophecy (noun)
prophesy (verb)
pursue
receipt
recommend
recurrence
relevance
relevant
remainder
remembrance
reminiscent
renaissance
repress
rhythm
secretary
separate

sergeant
shriek
siege
significance
skilful
stationary
stationery
stratum
subtlety
subtly
supersede
suppress
survivor
syllable
temperament
tendency
theoretic
tortuous
transferred
transience
truly
tyranny
undermine
unequivocally
unforgettable
unmanageable
unnecessary
unwieldy
variety
vengeance
vermilion
vicious

viscous
weird
wholly
withhold

such

When it means 'to a very great degree or extent', <u>such</u> is an over-used word. It should be used sparingly for emphasis: *such a mess, such an obedient dog, such an appalling play.*

<u>Such</u> is used with 'as' to mean 'of the sort already specified' or 'about to be specified':

I am going on safari but I don't know what to wear on a trip such as this.

He is not such a frightening person as he looks.

<u>Such as</u> can also mean 'for example':

New farm machinery such as tractors, combine harvesters and hedge trimmers have transformed the landscape.

'Like' should not be used instead of <u>such as</u> in a list of this sort. 'Like' properly precedes a comparison. (*New machines, like new clothes, last longer if you look after them.*)

<u>Such that</u> indicates an outcome or result:

The weight of the safe was such that the burglars could not lift it.

than

<u>Than</u> is usually a conjunction linking two items of comparison or contrast:

He always drives faster than his brother does.

I am healthier now than I was a year ago.

It can be a preposition when it is not followed by a stated or implied verb:

That cost me more than £50.

I could mow the lawn in less than an hour.

Care needs to be taken when a pronoun follows <u>than</u>. The correct form is indicated if the writer thinks what the implied verb is:

You are a better swimmer than me is wrong. It should be *You are a better swimmer than I* (*am* is implied).

You like children more than I (*do* is implied). But *You like children more than me* is correct if it means 'You like children more than you like me'. It is important to be clear about the intended meaning and to rephrase if there is a risk of ambiguity or misunderstanding.

see **as**

that, which

<u>That</u> and <u>which</u> can both introduce a restrictive/defining clause, that is one that is necessary to complete the meaning of the main clause. <u>That</u> should generally be first choice:

Those are the apples that/which come from Normandy.

Where is the old seat that/which used to be at the bottom of the garden?

A comma is not needed before a defining clause.

<u>Which</u> should be used to introduce a non-restrictive/non-defining clause, that is one that is not necessary to complete the meaning of the main clause:

The seaside piers, which were great Victorian structures, are now broken and disused.

The clause 'which . . . structures' could be removed without affecting the meaning of the rest of the sentence. Commas are needed to separate the non-defining clause from the main clause. They act like brackets.

see **parenthesis**

In a complex sentence, to avoid repetition, it is acceptable to replace <u>that</u> with <u>which</u>:

That was when we discovered that all the bridges which we had crossed on our journey had been built by Brunel.

and vice versa:

The car that stood in the garage facing the street that was called 40th Street and which led to the sea . . .

That as a conjunction can generally be omitted:

I know (that) he can be relied on.

It should be included if there is a danger of ambiguity:

I thought that yesterday he did not look well and *I thought yesterday that he did not look well* have slightly different meanings.

the *see* **a**

thence *see* **hence**

though *see* **although**

try and, try to

In writing, almost without exception, try to is preferred. Try and and try to are more or less equivalent in meaning, although some usages are distinctive.

Try and suggests greater drive and need for action:

Try and help her up while I go and fetch a chair.

'And' may only be used after try itself (but not after 'trying' or 'tried' which both require 'to').

In standard written English, try to suggests effort and endeavour:

If we are setting out early, we ought to try to get some sleep.

I shall try to change my library books tomorrow.

Try to should be used in negative constructions:

She wouldn't even try to help.

Won't you try to get here earlier?

type of *see* **kind of**

uninterested *see* **disinterested**

use, of use, no use

It is correct to use 'of' in sentences like:

Is this jacket of any use to you?

This skirt is too small to be of much use.

However, it is common practice, and acceptable, to omit 'of' in some contexts:

Is this old lawnmower (of) any use to you?

(Of) what use is it if it is not sharp?

used to

Used to can mean 'accustomed to' or 'did habitually':

I have got used to preparing my own sandwiches.

I used to go to the market every Friday.

In negatives and interrogatives used to can be ungainly. The auxiliary verb 'did' should be pressed into service:

There used to be a golf course near here, didn't there?

I didn't use to play golf very well, or *I used not to play golf very well.*

very *see* **many**

was, were

In some contexts, it can be difficult to choose between was and were. It is important to understand the difference between the past indicative was and the past subjunctive were.

Was is the past tense of 'is':

I was out late last night.

It was very difficult to decide what to do.

Was or were may be used when the suggestions at issue are factual, likely or just possible:

If he was/were to come to this country, his health would suffer.
If we suppose that he was/were not lying, then your case would collapse.

Use <u>was</u> when 'if' could be replaced by 'whether':
I doubt if/whether she was in a fit state to travel.
I do not know if/whether he was planning to see you.

<u>Were</u> is used in a conditional clause when the suggestions introduced are imaginary, non-factual or obviously untrue or unlikely:

If I were you, I would pay off the debt. (Imaginary: I am not you.)

If his father were a millionaire, he would have no trouble settling his debts. (The statement makes it obvious that his father is not a millionaire.)

<u>Were</u> is used when 'if' is followed by 'not':
If it were not (not *was not*) *for the children, we should have been in Spain by now.*

When a verb is preceded by 'as if' or 'as though':
He treats me as if/as though I were his servant.
and when a verb like 'wish' is followed by 'that':
I wish that he were taking my place.

<u>Were</u>, not <u>was</u>, is used when it opens a conditional sentence:
Were it not for the poor service, I would recommend this hotel.

Although '*if I were you*' and '*as it were*' are still widely used, <u>was</u> is increasingly displacing <u>were</u>.

see **moods**

which *see* **that**

while, whilst
<u>While</u> encloses the notion of time. It means 'at the same time as', 'during the time that', and is best used in a time context:
He arrived while I was in the bath.

While I was on holiday, my house caught fire.

More loosely, it can mean 'whereas' or 'although':

He wanted to live in the country while she preferred the city.

While Jake had the advantage in height, Crusher was much more agile.

It is important to avoid ambiguities:

She served lunch while he washed the dishes could mean that both played a part, or that he was washing dishes at the very time she was serving lunch. A different construction is needed if misunderstanding cannot be avoided.

Whilst has roughly the same meaning as while but it has an archaic feel and most contemporary writers would not use it. Whilst cannot take the place of 'and', 'but', or 'on the other hand'.

who, whom, whose, who's

These refer generally to people, but also to animals and things. Who is the subject of a verb:

The girl who won the championship was astounded.

Our cat, who is called Ethel, is black and white.

It was Germany who invented the autobahn.

Whom is the object of a verb or a preposition:

The doctor whom I consulted proved reassuring.

The patients to whom she gave a pep talk were very attentive.

To whom did you lend the book?

Whom have you met this morning?

As whom is in steady decline, those last two are more likely now to be:

Who did you lend the book to?

Who have you met this morning?

Whose means 'of whom', 'of which' and refers to both people and things:

This is the man whose shop was struck by lightning.
He delivered a speech whose purpose was to rally the troops.
<u>Who's</u> is an abbreviation of 'who is' or 'who has':
Who's for a run before breakfast?
This is the woman who's running for President.
Who's got the right answer?
There's the man who's run the marathon.

will *see* **shall**

would *see* **should**

would rather, had rather
<u>Would rather</u> is generally preferred to <u>had rather</u>. Both are idiomatically abbreviated to <u>'-d rather</u> (e.g. 'I'd rather', 'he'd rather', 'they'd rather').
Only <u>would rather</u> may be used in questions:
Would you rather have tea or a cold drink?

you
As a generalizing pronoun, meaning 'people at large', 'the general public', <u>you</u> is now much more commonly used than 'one': *When speaking in public, one should smile at one's audience* is much more likely to be *When speaking in public you should smile at your audience.*
You get very good value at that discount store.
When you fill in this form, make sure you have written your age in the proper place.
'One' can help to avoid confusion between the personal and the general use of <u>you</u> but the important thing is to be consistent and not to mix them.
see **one**

4. *Clear Grammar and Punctuation: How to name the parts of language*

—

When we listen to sports commentaries, we rely for understanding on our knowledge of the technical terms and the 'shorthand' commentators use to describe the action ('off-side', 'penalty', 'foot fault', 'maiden over', 'knock on', 'touchdown', and so on). Most of us have picked up their meanings in one way or another as we have grown up.

Language, too, has its technical terms and these are listed alphabetically in this chapter. Just knowing these terms will not guarantee to help us write clearer English, but they are the tools, the labels, we use when discussing and discovering ways of improving how we write in terms of both effect and clarity.

We use constructions, named by these terms, daily without realizing that we are speaking and writing **prose**, or that, as here, we use a **linking verb**, an **adjectival phrase**, a correctly placed **adverb** and a **noun clause**, along with other parts of speech. The labels can help us to pinpoint easily and quickly the difficulties and opportunities which the writing process creates. The terms, then, are not the end but the means to the end.

absolute adjectives *see* **adjectives**

abstract nouns *see* **nouns**

active voice *see* **verbs**

adjectives
An <u>adjective</u> is any word which modifies a noun or noun equivalent. It restricts or extends the meaning of the

person, place or thing named by the noun by telling us more about it.

'Tent' will serve as an example: the adjectives used can describe its special attributes (*a spacious tent*) and qualities (*a waterproof tent*), indicate ownership (*your tent*), limit by reducing possibilities (*that tent, Kate's tent*) or extend by giving more information (*our larger waterproof nylon tent*).

Most adjectives are gradable, that is they can be used in a positive, comparative and superlative form (*a large tent; a larger tent; the largest tent*). Some cannot take -er and -est, but instead are preceded by 'more' and 'most' (*a more robust tent; the most robust tent*).

Absolute adjectives are those which cannot be used comparatively or superlatively. They express a final and complete quality in the nouns they modify. Examples include 'perfect', 'entire', 'flawless', 'unique', 'total'; you cannot describe something as 'more perfect' or 'most unique' (though it is common in informal spoken English). However, absolute adjectives can be modified by the adverbs 'almost' and 'nearly':

Leonardo could draw an almost perfect circle freehand.

A passerby sent a nearly flawless vase crashing to the floor.

Classifying adjectives are used to identify someone or something as being of a particular class or kind: we write about *a wooden spoon, an Indian mystic, a social service, an industrial depression, metal nutcrackers*, etc. When used like this, these adjectives have no comparative or superlative form: we do not write about *a more wooden spoon, a most industrial depression*, and so on.

The order in which adjectives are used follows a convention: qualitative – colour – classifying:

Our little grey home in the west.

A majestic, golden, Lombardy poplar.

However, <u>classifying adjectives</u> which are not gradable and denoting shape often precede colour:

He laid an oval green lawn.

We admired the cylindrical white pillars of the bridge.

We need an elliptical green plastic pot for the hyacinths.

Where more than one <u>classifying adjective</u> appears before a noun, the following order should be followed: age – shape – nationality – material:

This is a 12th-century spiral staircase.

She brought back a Breton lace tablecloth.

He auctioned a 19th-century round English metal paper-weight.

<u>Comparative</u> and <u>superlative adjectives</u> precede all others:

He was one of the older, more versatile, music-hall comedians.

These must be the lowest annual untaxed profits so far recorded.

In a succession of descriptive words and phrases, the elements should be arranged in a growing order of importance:

It was not a helpful, kind, necessary or true account.

If there is no clear reason for adopting a particular order, start with the shortest word and end with the longest.

see **comma**

adverbs

Adverbs modify verbs, adjectives and other adverbs whether these are single words, phrases or whole clauses: *sailing dangerously, positively dangerous, extremely dangerously, sailing at an even speed, Evidently, she likes dangerous living.*

Generally, <u>adverbs</u> are preceded by 'more' and 'most' to form the comparative and superlative ending: *easily, more easily, most easily.* Some, however, take -er and -est: *soon, sooner, soonest.*

antecedent *see* **pronoun**

apposition

Apposition is the use of a word or phrase which, without a conjunction, stands next to another word or phrase and gives more information about it: *my brother, James* (*James* is in apposition to *my brother*); *This little car, the most reliable I ever possessed, was won in a raffle* (*the most . . . possessed* is in apposition to *This little car*).

articles *see* **a, an, the**

auxiliary verbs *see* **verbs**

base form of verb

This is the infinitive form of any verb as it is found in a dictionary without inflections. It is often preceded by 'to' (*to jump, to think, to radiate, to report*) when it is called the to-infinitive.

   see **verbs**

case

This is the form of a noun, pronoun or adjective which shows its relationship to another word. It may be subjective or nominative (*He drinks water* – *He* is subjective/nominative); objective or accusative (*Give him water* – *him* is objective/accusative); or genitive (*His drinking is moderate* – *his* is genitive).

classifying adjectives *see* **adjectives**

clause

A clause includes a subject and a finite form of a verb. It may be independent (or main), co-ordinate or subordinate.

   see **sentences**

collective nouns *see* **nouns**

colloquial

A style of writing that is composed of fragments, words or phrases, used in everyday conversation, is called <u>colloquial</u>. It is often racy, elliptical, always unprepared and even slangy. It is more naturally suited to speech than to writing and there is no firm borderline between the <u>colloquial</u> and the informal.

complement

A <u>complement</u> is a word or group of words (nouns, pronouns, adjectives) which follow a linking verb, such as 'be', 'become', 'seem', 'appear', 'look', etc. and give more information about the subject or object of the verb. They are necessary to complete the point of the sentence:

He became impatient. (Impatient is a *complement*.)

She seemed tired and depressed.

It looked fiercely at the intruder.

One day he will make a good attacking forward.

Sorry, it's me again.

conjunctions

There are three types of <u>conjunction</u> which link words or groups of words.

<u>Co-ordinating conjunctions</u> link elements that are co-ordinate, that is of similar grammatical importance. They are 'and', 'but', 'for', 'or', 'nor', 'yet' (*ham and eggs*; *cheerless but willing*; *if we sink or if we swim*; *He always did his best yet never managed to save any money*).

<u>Correlative conjunctions</u> are formed by pairs of words like 'either . . . or', 'neither . . . nor', 'so . . . as', 'whether . . . or', 'both . . . and', 'not only . . . but also' ('also' is sometimes omitted). Neither element in a statement makes sense on its own and requires the other part to be complete:

Either he will arrive on time or postpone his visit until tomorrow.

Whether you come or not doesn't concern me.

He not only broke his rod but (also) failed to catch any fish.

A subordinating conjunction joins a subordinate clause (one which has less grammatical importance) to a main clause (one that can stand alone and is not dependent on any other):

He was annoyed because the ferry had already gone. He was annoyed is the main clause (it makes sense on its own); *because* is the subordinating conjunction introducing the subordinate clause (*because the ferry had already gone*), which is subordinate to the main clause and dependent on it for its meaning.

co-ordinating conjunctions *see* **conjunctions**

correlative conjunctions *see* **conjunctions**

count nouns *see* **nouns**

demonstrative pronouns *see* **pronouns**

determiner

A determiner is a word used before a noun to indicate whether it refers to the specific or the general. Determiners which refer to things the reader knows or may be assumed to know include: 'the', 'this', 'that', 'these', 'those', 'my', 'your', 'his', 'her', 'its', 'our', 'their'. Those which refer to things the reader cannot be assumed to know or which have not been already mentioned include: 'a', 'an', 'all', 'any', 'both', 'each', 'either', 'neither', 'every', 'more', 'most', 'fewer', 'no', 'other', 'several', 'some'.

He raised his cap when he had scored a century.

Many spectators stood up and cheered.

see **a, an, the**

direct object

The direct object is the noun or noun cluster in a sentence or clause which designates the person or thing acted upon by a transitive verb:

I ate a hot meal. (*A hot meal* is the direct object.)

double negative

In its simplest form, a <u>double negative</u> is easy to spot and to avoid. The main reason for not using it is that the second negative cancels out the first and the statement becomes meaningless:

I haven't got no money technically means 'I have got money', which is not the meaning intended.

Some sentences contain semi-negative adverbs (such as 'barely', 'hardly', 'scarcely') which cannot be associated with another negative word:

I haven't got hardly any money is wrong and should be *I have got hardly any money* or *I have hardly any money.*

He couldn't scarcely reach the top shelf should be *He could scarcely reach the top shelf.*

Sometimes 'not' is used with a negative form as a stylistic device or to refine meaning:

It is not unlikely is not quite the same as *It is likely.*

It is not uncommon for walkers to lose their way on the hills suggests that this fate befalls walkers but perhaps not very often, whereas *It is common for walkers to lose their way in the hills* is a much more emphatic statement and implies that it happens all the time.

Another acceptable, colloquial and now idiomatic use is:

I shouldn't be surprised if it didn't rain before dark which appears to mean that the writer would not be surprised if it did not rain before dark but, in fact, means the writer would not be surprised if it <u>did</u> rain before dark.

finite verb
The <u>finite</u> is the form which shows the tense and subject of a <u>verb</u>:

We'll push the car to get it started.

I thought it was in my back pocket.

They think their plan is very clever, but they have overlooked one thing.

see **verbs**

formal writing
The term <u>formal writing</u> suggests to some a stilted, even stuffy style. Instead, it refers to a need for careful preparation and measured presentation. It is most often to be found in news bulletins on national radio and television, in articles and editorials in the quality press (newspapers and magazines) and in reports of professional bodies and the journals of learned societies.

gerund
The <u>gerund</u> is the '-ing' form of any verb

see **verbs**

gradable adjectives *see* **adjectives**

historic present
When the present tense of a verb is used to describe past events, its use is described as the <u>historic present</u>. Used sparingly, it can add impact to an account of events and is popular with thriller writers. It is not suitable for formal writing:

Midnight. He is standing under a street lamp. Lightning flashes. A car approaches.

imperative mood *see* **moods**

impersonal verbs *see* **verbs**

indefinite pronouns *see* **pronouns**

indicative mood *see* **moods**

indirect object
The <u>indirect object</u> is the second object of some transitive verbs. It is a noun or noun group that shows to or for whom the action of the verb takes place:

Will you tell us a story? (*us* is the indirect object; *a story* is the direct object; *tell* is the transitive verb.)

Give the earthquake victims all the assistance you can. (*You* is the understood subject; *give* is the transitive verb; *all the assistance* is the direct object; *the earthquake victims* is the indirect object.)

see **direct object**

infinitive *see* **base form of verb**

informal writing
The normal, everyday manner of communicating, relaxed and easily understood, is described as <u>informal</u>. It is the language of debate, discussion, argument and opinion.

see **formal writing**

interjection
An <u>interjection</u> is an exclamatory word or phrase used to express sudden excitement, surprise, pleasure, anger, horror, etc. It stands independently in a sentence. Examples include *Oh, dear! Damn! How awful!*

interrogative pronouns *see* **pronouns**

intransitive verb
An <u>intransitive verb</u> has only a subject, no direct or indirect object and has no passive form:

She slept quietly.

I have been waiting for more than an hour.

jargon

Originally, <u>jargon</u> was the term used to describe the specialist language used by and among people who have an interest in common, where the terminology they use is unfamiliar to, and may not be understood by, the rest of us. It is most often applied to work-related words, expressions, etc. and is sometimes intended to 'exclude' those who do not understand it. More recently, <u>jargon</u> has come to be used to describe the euphemisms, clichés and empty rhetoric which groups deliberately use to mislead or evade questions. Avoid jargon by checking and rechecking that your language is clear, direct and simple to understand.

linking verbs *see* **verbs**

modals

Also known as modal auxiliaries and modal verbs, <u>modals</u> are used in verbal groups to express possibility, intention, necessity, recommendation, permission, etc. They include 'can', 'could', 'may', 'might', 'must', 'ought', 'shall', 'should', 'will', 'would'. <u>Modals</u> are followed only by the infinitive verb, that is, the base form, sometimes preceded by 'to':

You can stay; I might turn up; They must be there; I ought to leave.

modifier

A <u>modifier</u> is a word or group of words which come before another word to alter and govern its meaning:

This is a happy day.
That was an unfortunate and expensive lawsuit.
He made a clear, helpful suggestion.
see **qualifier**

moods

Verbs have three <u>moods</u> which indicate an attitude on the part of the writer to what is being written and to the reader:

The <u>indicative mood</u> is the most common. It simply states facts and asks questions:

I met John and Marion yesterday.

Shall I prepare a meal?

The <u>imperative mood</u> is one of command, direction and entreaty:

Come round and listen carefully.

Close the door behind you.

The <u>subjunctive mood</u> has traditionally expressed wishes, hopes, non-factual situations, and unreal conditions rather than actual ones. Its use has declined and there are now few occasions when 'were' is used. (*I wish I were able to do that.*) Such use can sound stilted and archaic (*I wish I were a million miles from here! Far be it from me . . .; On your head be it; Come what may*). Informally, 'was' is replacing 'were' but this is disapproved of for writing.

see **was, were**

The <u>subjunctive</u> is often replaced by auxiliary verbs and conditionals like 'may', 'might', 'should':

I recommend that he employs another solicitor (indicative).

I recommend that he employ another solicitor (subjunctive).

I recommend that he should employ another solicitor.

I recommend that he ought to employ another solicitor.

see **modals**

The <u>subjunctive</u> should follow 'if' where a hypothetical position is suggested:

If I were in your place, I shouldn't go.

but not when 'if' suggests a position that is likely or possible:

If that was his reason for leaving, he could have told us.

The subjunctive should not be used after 'whether' or 'if' when it means 'whether':

He rang to ask whether I was going to the cinema.

James wondered if Alison was present at the meeting.

non-finite verbs *see* **verbs**

nouns

Nouns are used to name a person, place, thing, feeling or quality. They are generally classed according to how they are being used.

Count nouns refer to things which are countable. They have a singular and plural form and, when singular, are always preceded by a determiner ('a', 'an' or 'the') (*see* **determiner**). They are usually concrete, that is concerned with physical objects and the real world.

Uncount nouns refer to things that are not divisible into separate units but have bulk, quantity, stuff. They have only a singular form and preceding determiners are rarely used. They are generally abstract and concerned with feelings, qualities or concepts, and the spiritual, rather than physical objects in the material world.

It is possible to count numbers of jackets, trousers, shirts and coats (these are count nouns), but impossible to count 'clothing' (which is an uncount noun).

It is possible to count ideas, theories, theses, concepts, but impossible to count 'philosophy'.

Proper nouns are names (mostly beginning with a capital letter) of particular people (John, Mozart, Picasso), places (Oxford, Devon, Ghana), things by brand name (Drambuie, Marmite), institutions (Parliament, Scotland Yard) and titles (The Sunday Times, Hamlet). Most do not require a determiner. Some are always preceded by 'The', usually also with a capital first letter (The Salvation Army, The United States, The Times).

Singular nouns are only ever used in the singular, need a determiner and a singular verb. (*The blame is entirely mine. I recall the past by keeping a diary.*)

Plural nouns have only a plural form, may or may not require a determiner and take a plural verb. (*The trousers are too long. We'll need a pair of pliers to unscrew that. I'll just mend this tear in my jeans.*) They may be preceded by 'some'.

Collective nouns refer to collections or groups of people, animals and things. A collective noun may require a singular or plural verb according to how its usage is understood:

The committee is meeting this morning and has to come to a decision. (The committee is seen as a group of individuals acting collectively as one unit.)

The committee were not agreed how they should reply to the offer made to them. (The committee contains individuals some of whom think one thing, others another. They are therefore seen as individuals.)

Whatever choice of verb is made, consistency is vital. It is important to avoid *The committee is meeting this morning and have to come to a decision.*

parenthesis

A parenthesis (often referred to in its plural form 'parentheses') is an additional comment or explanation introduced into a sentence and marked off by commas, brackets or dashes:

My favourite opera, Mozart's 'Don Giovanni', is on at the moment.

The colours (blue, pink and yellow) clashed horribly.

Your last question – about taxation policy – completely stumped him.

125

Some kinds of <u>parentheses</u> could grammatically stand alone:
I read your letter – you really shouldn't use pink writing paper – and was delighted to learn that Jack had won first prize.

This last form should be used sparingly as over-use can be very irritating. It suggests that the writer's work is full of afterthoughts and hesitations.

Square brackets are used when a writer quotes someone else and adds or includes an explanatory comment of his or her own:
My teacher said, 'Take this disgusting thing [my pet snake] out of my classroom at once'.

participles
These are two forms of a verb used to make different tenses. The <u>past participle</u>, preceded by 'I have', 'you had', etc. is the base form plus -ed, or a different form with irregular verbs.

see **verbs**

The <u>present participle</u> always ends with -ing and is used for continuous (progressive) tenses: *I am eating breakfast; I was singing in the bath; I had been shopping all morning.*

parts of speech
The <u>parts of speech</u> are adjective, adverb, conjunction, interjection, noun, preposition, pronoun and verb. A word is classified according to its role in a sentence. A word may appear as different <u>parts of speech</u> although it has exactly the same form:
It was cool and dark in the doorway (cool is an adjective).
We took refuge in the cool of the doorway (noun).
Let the coffee cool a little before you drink it (verb).

passive voice *see* **verbs**

perfect infinitive

The <u>perfect infinitive</u> is the verb form preceded by 'to have'. It is often incorrectly used after a perfect tense:

I should have liked to have painted that picture is wrong and should be *I should like to have painted`that picture* (to express how I feel in the present) or *I should have liked to paint that picture* (to express how I used to feel). In neither case is it necessary to have two past tenses. One is enough. This construction can cause a lot of difficulty and is best avoided if possible.

personal pronoun *see* **pronoun**

phrasal verbs *see* **verbs**

phrase

A <u>phrase</u> is a group of words without a subject and predicate and therefore not a complete clause: *in the middle of the street; the farmer in the dell; in the nick of time.*

plural nouns *see* **nouns**

predicate

The <u>predicate</u> is the part of a sentence or clause which says something about the subject:

He (subject) *decided to go swimming* (predicate).

A herd of ponies (subject) *galloped across the moor* (predicate).

preposition

Literally meaning something which is put in front of something else, a <u>preposition</u> is a word placed before a noun or pronoun to introduce and form a phrase which modifies another word or phrase in the sentence. <u>Prepositions</u> usually show relationships between one thing and another in time, place, manner, reason, etc.:

Before the shops close . . . (*Before* is a preposition.)

. . . *after the wedding.* (*After* is a preposition.)

With great difficulty . . . (*With* is a preposition.)

Prepositions always take an object, but need not be placed before their objects. Ending a sentence with a preposition is fundamental to some idiomatic English expressions (even if strictly grammatically incorrect):

What has he been up to? sounds ridiculous as *Up to what has he been?*

Who do you want to speak to? sounds more natural and less stilted than *To whom do you want to speak?*

pronoun

A <u>pronoun</u> takes the place of a noun or noun phrase that has already been used (which is called the 'antecedent'). The <u>pronoun</u> must agree with its antecèdent in gender, number and form (this last applies to <u>personal pronouns</u>, like 'my', 'his', 'your', etc.).

John has taken his dog for a walk.

<u>Personal pronouns</u> (except 'you' and 'it') have subject ('I', 'we', 'he', 'she', 'they'), object ('me', 'us', 'him', 'her', 'them') and possessive ('my', 'our', 'his', 'her', 'their') forms.

<u>Reflexive pronouns</u> refer to the same person or thing as the subject and are 'myself', 'yourself', 'himself', 'herself', 'itself', 'ourselves', 'yourselves', 'themselves'.

<u>Relative pronouns</u> introduce adjective or noun clauses. They are 'who' (subjective), 'whom' (objective), 'whose' (possessive), 'which', 'that' (plural).

<u>Indefinite pronouns</u> refer to general, undefined people and things. They include 'all', 'few', 'many', 'everybody', 'anyone',

'nobody', 'none', 'someone', 'something', 'both', 'each'. They cannot have a determiner. It is important not to confuse the pronoun and the adjective forms:

Few are required to attend classes every day (pronoun).

Few students are required to attend classes every day (adjective).

<u>Demonstrative pronouns</u>, when they stand alone, designate a definite or specific person or thing ('this', 'that', 'these', 'those'). It is important not to confuse the pronoun and the adjective forms:

Give me a box of those (pronoun).

Give me a box of those chocolates (adjective).

<u>Interrogative pronouns</u> ask questions – 'who', 'whom', 'whose', 'which', 'what'.

proper nouns *see* **nouns**

Punctuation
apostrophe
The <u>apostrophe</u> is used to denote possession with nouns and pronouns, and to distinguish singular from plural. In singular words the <u>apostrophe</u> precedes the final -s and follows the -s of regular plurals.

a week's holiday; ten weeks' holiday.

Irregular plurals are treated as singular:

the men's room; the women's club; the mice's love of cheese.

Proper nouns which end with -s add -'s:

Brahms's symphonies; Dickens's universal appeal.

The <u>apostrophe</u> can be used to indicate that something is missing:

it's (for *it is* or *it has*); *didn't* (for *did not*); *they're* (for *they are*).

In writing the full form is preferable. The apostrophe never appears in 'ours', 'yours', 'hers', 'theirs', etc.

There is no apostrophe in 'its' meaning 'belongs to it'. Its use is a common error: *I can't make out its shape.*

see **its, it's**

brackets

Like double dashes, brackets are always used in pairs for focusing on extra information, afterthoughts and asides:

Ballpoint pens (which used to be known as 'Biros') first arrived in Britain in the 1940s.

Perhaps he will apologize or perhaps (as usual) he won't.

Brackets are also used to enclose cross references and parallels:

For putting on a veneer (see diagram) you need a different adhesive.

The midday temperature was 16°C (that is 61°F).

see **parenthesis**

capital letters

Capital letters are used as follows:

- to begin the first word in a sentence
- to begin any complete sentence within quotation marks (*He said, 'This milk is sour'. But, 'The best cheese my mother makes,' he said, 'is from goat's milk.'* There is no capital letter on *is* because it continues the sentence before *he said.*)
- for proper nouns see **proper nouns**
- for days of the week, months of the year, festivals (like Christmas, Easter), historical periods (Jurassic, Elizabethan, Renaissance), signs of the Zodiac (Taurus, Libra), place names (houses, streets, villages, towns, cities, counties, countries, continents, seas, oceans, deserts, etc.), races and nationalities
- for the pronoun 'I' (but not for 'me', 'my', 'mine')

- for people's titles when they precede the name (Ms Pavrinder, Dr Livingstone, Lord Palmerston, Queen Elizabeth) and abbreviations of titles which follow people's names (J.P., M.P., M.B.E., etc.)
- for the first word and all the important words in titles of any kind (*The Mill on the Floss*, Desert Island Discs, Top of the Pops)
- for institutions and businesses, and the names of ships and aircraft (The Royal Shakespeare Company, Harrods, The Bank of England, *Ark Royal*, Concorde)
- for religious references (God, Judaism, Islam)

colon (:)

Colons are used:

- to express a balanced contrast without using a conjunction (*Speech is silver: silence is golden*)
- to introduce a phrase or clause which offers more information or comment on what has gone before, sometimes in contrasting form (*An interesting question is how he got in here: a more interesting one is how he got out.*)
- to introduce lists (*These are the items you will need: stout boots, thick socks, a warm sweater and gloves.*)
- to stress what has already been said (*I firmly reject the findings of the report: reject them altogether.*)
- to introduce long, indented quotations, especially if they are not within quotation marks
- to introduce speech in plays (*Fibbs: Well now, Wills, I've heard there's been a lot of trouble in the factory. Wills: Yes I . . . suppose you could call it that, Mr Fibbs. From Trouble in the Works by Harold Pinter (1959)*

131

comma (,)

commas are used:

- to make pauses in a long sentence and to divide it into simpler parts so that the meaning is more readily understood (*We busied ourselves with fishing the rock pools, searching for stones with a hole right through them, gathering shells and rubbery seaweed, and beachcombing rigorously all through the summer.*)

- to separate words, phrases or clauses in a list or series (*The lay-by was littered with old mattresses, bedsteads, plastic bottles, beer cans and broken glass; He got up, shaved, showered, dressed quickly and left the house.*) The comma before 'and' is often omitted unless there is a risk of ambiguity. (*We planted cuttings of red, yellow, mauve and white carnations.* Are there carnations of three colours or four? If three — one a mixture of mauve and white — there is no comma before 'and'; if four, there should be.) The comma is omitted when one adjective describes another next to it (*a fine gold necklace; a deep purple bruise*).

- to mark off main clauses, in particular long and elaborate ones, linked by a conjunction like 'and', 'but', 'or', etc. (*We had intended to see a bull fight yesterday before returning to our camp, but Jack was completely overcome by sunstroke, and we were forced to call off that part of the programme.*)

- to set apart a participial phrase (*Hearing a movement in the unlit cellar, he froze with terror.*)

- between very short clauses not linked by conjunctions (*We considered the options, we settled the priorities, we forecast the reaction, we decided to act.*)

- to set apart a tag question from the rest of a sentence (*You have read today's paper, haven't you?*)

- before and after a clause or phrase that provides extra but inconsequential matter about the noun it follows (*The daffodil bulbs, which we bought from a little shop in Broad Street, have given us the finest show of spring flowers we have ever had.*) Restrictive, or defining, adjectival clauses are not separated from the sentence by <u>commas</u>. (*The daffodil bulbs that we bought from Woolworths have produced the finest show in the garden. Our attention is drawn to the Woolworth bulbs, not to any others in the garden.*)
  see **that, which**
- to set apart a word, phrase or clause that introduces and applies to the sentence as a whole (*Needless to say, I don't believe him. However, we had never seen her before; By and large, I agree with you.*)
  see **sentence adverbs**
- to set apart the name or appellation of a person being addressed, or an interjection (*What do you think of the climb, Tom?; Sir, welcome to the hotel; Confound it, the toast has burnt again.*)

dash (–)

A single <u>dash</u> is used:

- to focus on a swift change of thought: (*What we saw when we opened the front door – well I'll spare you the details.*)
- to draw together items in a list (*Poetry, drama, novels, literary criticism, social essays – D.H. Lawrence's legacy to 20th-century literature.*)
- to give emphasis to a repeated word (*The game was ruined by the number and ferocity of deliberate fouls – fouls that it is shameful to be compelled to record.*)
- to avoid writing someone's name in full and to stand in for a swear word (*Mrs G– has a lot to answer for over the*

133

vote rigging.) (*I don't care a – what you – well think*). Graffiti writers ignore this convention and write in full.

A double <u>dash</u> is used to enclose a parenthesis instead of brackets or double commas

> *I've just called at 'The Blue Angel' — that's our favourite eating place — to book a table for tomorrow evening.*

see **parenthesis**

exclamation mark (!)

The <u>exclamation mark</u> is used at the end of a sentence or phrase to indicate forceful, demonstrative feelings of anger, elation, surprise, pleasure, etc. It should be used very sparingly and not in pairs or triplets:

> *What a brilliant present! Look out! You idiot! What a relief!*

The exclamation mark has its own full stop and never needs another one.

full stop (.)

Also called a full point, or period (in American English), the <u>full stop</u> is used as follows:

- to mark the end of a sentence which is not a question or an exclamation. (*A sentence is a word or group of words containing a main verb and making complete sense.*)
- to mark an abbreviation (*i.e., e.g., no.* (for number), *etc.*). Where the abbreviation ends with the same letter as the original word, modern usage accepts that a full stop is not needed (*Mr* for Mister, *Dr* for Doctor, *St* for Saint, etc.).
- in abbreviations formed from initial capital letters. When the abbreviation becomes very well known, however (*BBC, USA, UN, RAF*), the full stops are often omitted.
- to keep the numbers in dates and times apart for clarity (*27896* is just a sequence of numbers, but *27.8.96* conveys 27 August 1996; *20.35* is 8.35pm), and to mark

the decimal point in amounts of money (£2.55) and metric measurements (6.5 metres)

- to establish a break or gap, usually when quoting another piece of writing by a series of three stops to acknowledge the omission (*He then went on to prove his point . . . and finally arrived at his recommendations.*)
- to indicate hesitation (*I wish to say . . . er, thank you . . . to our . . . er . . .*), etc.

question mark [?]

The <u>question mark</u> has its own full stop and does not need another one. It is used as follows:

- to take the place of a full stop at the end of direct question sentences, that is when the actual words spoken are given (*May I have another cup of coffee? When do you expect to get here?*)
- at the end of the actual words quoted when part of a sentence (*'Shall I get a copy of the Guardian as well?', he asked.*)
- in dialogue at the end of a sentence which is not a question but which expresses surprise, interest, incredulity, etc. (*She's not really going to swim the Channel? And she is actually planning to pass that off as genuine?*)

When quotation marks are used, the <u>question mark</u> should be placed immediately before the last quotation mark and when another writer's question is quoted, the question mark is part of the quotation and must come before the closing quotation mark:

'Have you left the tin-opener at home, Bob?'

'If Winter comes, can Spring be far behind?' (Shelley)

If the question mark is not part of the quotation, it must be placed outside the quotation marks:

Will you not agree with me that 'The man who makes no mistakes does not usually make anything'?

● to indicate that a conjecture is dubious and should not be regarded as fact: *Oliver Goldsmith (?1730–74)* indicates that his exact date of birth is uncertain or unknown; a seedling labelled *'Cyclamen ?white'* expresses uncertainty about its variety, at least until it flowers when the matter will be settled.

The <u>question mark</u> is not used with indirect questions, that is in reporting what another person has asked but not using the actual words spoken:

Bob asked Mary if she would arrive in time for lunch.

quotation marks (' or ")

Single or double <u>quotation marks</u> are used when reporting the exact words which someone has said. They open and close the quotation and do not contain any other part of the sentence:

'I want you to stay at home,' my mother said.

'Are you coming with us?' she asked.

<u>Quotation marks</u> are also used to draw particular attention to a word or group of words often with a hint of mockery or irony:

He thinks he's a real 'champion'.

The use of single or double quotation marks is a matter of preference. It is important not to mix them in a piece of writing except to indicate a quote within a quote:

'I think it was Shakespeare who said "All the world's a stage", wasn't it?'

semi-colon (;)

A <u>semi-colon</u> is better than a comma for separating items in a list, especially if the individual items are fairly long or already contain commas:

As the smoke cleared we saw the damage: great slabs of rock, bright, clean, tilted on edge; rock dust settling and sifting in dry cascades; shrubs, torn from the rock face, hanging leafless with roots in the air.

It can also show the close relation between parts of a sentence, each of which could have been a sentence in its own right, but which are kept together to avoid the sharp division created by a full stop:

I shall enjoy my daily glass of orange juice; my daily swim; my weekly round of golf.

A <u>semi-colon</u> is always placed within a sentence, never at the end, and often before a clause or phrase introduced by a linking adverb like 'yet', 'nevertheless', 'moreover', 'otherwise', 'indeed', 'even so', 'therefore', etc.:

I haven't been able to find the book you asked for; nevertheless, I shall keep on trying.

He lost heavily on the Stock Market; even so, he seems as cheerful as ever.

slash mark (/)

Also called an oblique, solidus or stroke, the <u>slash mark</u> can be used:

- to separate alternatives (*Please write down your hobbies/ pastimes/interests in the appropriate box; We are serving crème brûlée and/or cheese, Madam.*)
- to affirm that both of two alternatives are acceptable (*. . . of paramount/supreme importance: 300 gm/11 oz of flour*)
- to mean 'or' (*A teacher soon learns the character of his/her pupils.*)
- to separate the numbers in dates (*25/12/96*), telephone numbers (*01234/67890*) and fractions (*1/2*)

qualifier

A <u>qualifier</u> is a word or group of words coming after a noun or pronoun to augment and govern its meaning (*in the flat below; the icing on the cake; one of the only models available; a bomb capable of destroying all mankind*).

reflexive pronouns *see* **pronouns**

relative clauses
These are subordinate clauses that tell us more about someone or something in the main (independent) clause. They can precede, follow, or come in the middle of, the main clause:

When I return, I'll tell you all the details.

He is the man who directed me to the station.

My puppy, which was given to me as a present, has become a great entertainer.

Relative clauses should be introduced by the relative pronouns, 'that', 'which' and, for people, nearly always 'who' or 'whom':

A man whom I met on holiday last year told me.

A man that I met on holiday last year told me.

or by relative conjunctions like 'when', 'where', 'because', 'since', 'while', 'although', etc.

see **that, which**

relative pronouns *see* **pronouns**

restrictive and non-restrictive clauses
A restrictive clause (also known as a defining clause) identifies precisely what is being modified and is introduced by the relative pronoun 'that' or 'which' ('that' is strongly preferred):

The chisel that is on the edge of the bench is the one I need. (This identifies the particular chisel and excludes any other chisels on the bench.)

The clause is not separated from its main clause by commas.

A <u>non-restrictive clause</u> (or non-defining clause) gives information of an incidental, non-defining kind. It is introduced by the relative pronoun 'which':

The motor car, which is a wonderful invention, will soon disappear from our roads. (This does not define any particular car and includes all cars generally.)

This type of clause is separated from its main clause by commas.

see **that, which**

sentence adverbs

These are single adverbs, or groups of words with adverbial force, that apply to a sentence or clause as a whole, not to parts of it. They usually come at the beginning of a sentence, and often express or reveal the writer's viewpoint on the opinion, statement, etc. that follows:

Luckily, I had crossed over the bridge just in time.

Strange as it may seem, I still enjoy taking exercise.

singular nouns *see* verbs

split infinitive

The infinitive is the base form of the verb, that is it has no letters added to the end and is not a past tense form; it is often used with 'to' before and next to it. A <u>split infinitive</u> occurs when an adverb or adverb phrase is inserted between 'to' and the base verb – one of the best known examples is *Star Trek's* 'To boldly go . . .'

There is no rule that a <u>split infinitive</u> should never be used, but it is so widely disliked that it is best avoided.

Finding a better position for the adverb can alter meaning and lead to ambiguity and awkwardness:

He was trying to gradually reduce his weight (split infinitive).

He was trying to reduce his weight gradually suggests he was trying to lose weight slowly.

He was trying gradually to reduce his weight implies that the 'trying' was gradual. This might also be *He was gradually trying to reduce his weight.*

There are now occasions when split infinitives are acceptable, for example when they simply sound right, or when an unexpected or unaccustomed importance is conferred on the adverb (*to fully understand; to really and thoroughly enjoy oneself; to openly admit; to deliberately and openly disobey*).

subjunctive moods *see* **moods**

subordinating conjunctions *see* **conjunctions**

tag, tag question
A tag question is a short clause (an auxiliary verb and a pronoun) at the end of a positive statement which changes it into a question:
She was born in Scotland, wasn't she?

tautology
Tautology is the needless repetition of the same sense in different words or phrases when they are adjacent or close:
He said he was writing the autobiography of his life.
First and foremost . . .
. . . a free gift.

to infinitive *see* **base form of verb**

transitive verbs *see* **verbs**

uncount nouns *see* **nouns**

verbs
Verbs can be made to express the whole array of time, past, present and future, by tenses; they depict action or existence and assert something about their subjects:

Joe is an expert fisherman. He is selling fish today, sold a large amount last week and will sell more next Friday. He has been selling fish for over thirty years.

<u>Linking verbs</u> link their subjects to a complement, an adjective or noun group telling us more about the subject. In *Joe is an expert fisherman*, 'is' brings about an equivalence between 'Joe' and 'expert fisherman', that is between subject and complement.

The <u>verb</u> 'to be' in one of its forms is most widely used, but others which act similarly include 'appear', 'become', 'come', 'look', 'remain', 'seem', 'stay'.

<u>Auxiliary verbs</u> serve little purpose on their own but are used with <u>main</u> (<u>lexical</u>) <u>verbs</u> to create a purposeful group. 'Be' and 'have' help to form tenses: 'be' is also used in passive constructions; and 'do' is generally used only for emphasis:

I am looking for a 50p piece which I dropped.

They have all been helping in the search.

I have been helped in the search.

I do mean it. I don't think about it.

Do you want me to buy a ticket?

Other <u>auxiliary verbs</u> are the <u>modal verbs</u> 'may', 'might', 'can', 'could', etc.

Forms of 'be' and 'have' (in the sense of possessing) are themselves sometimes <u>main verbs</u>:

I am your fairy godmother.

He has a large collection of books on sport.

<u>Impersonal verbs</u>, sometimes called '<u>weather verbs</u>', invariably have 'it' as their subject:

It looks like snow to me.

Is it still raining?

There is always an alternative way of expressing the same thing:

Snow is forecast, I believe.

Is the rain still falling?

<u>Phrasal verbs</u> combine with an adverb, a preposition, or both, to express a single meaning: *to stand down* (to withdraw); *to stand up for* (to support); *to stand in for* (to substitute or replace); *to stand out* (to be striking and noticeable); *to stand out for* (to delay reaching agreement), and so on. They are used widely in idiomatic language.

The <u>finite verb</u> changes its form to agree with the subject of its clause in person (first, second or third) and in number (singular or plural), and to indicate tense:

I drive; she drives; we drove; they have driven.

<u>Non-finite verbs</u> include infinitives and participles:

I photographed all the plans (finite verb).

He was unwise to photograph all the plans (non-finite verb).

The dockers gathered round their leader.

The clouds were gathering above the hills.

I am not a strong man since my accident.

I used to be a strong man before my accident.

<u>-ing verbs</u> are used in continuous tenses (*She was playing the piano*), as adjectives (*Her playing technique has improved*) or as a gerund, a verbal noun (*Her playing was quite outstanding*).

The <u>active voice</u> of a <u>transitive verb</u> describes the subject as doing something to or acting upon the object:

The foreman sacked him.

In the <u>passive voice</u> the object becomes the subject, and the subject the object:

He was sacked by the foreman.

<u>Transitive verbs</u> require a direct object to complete the sense and can be active or passive:

He drove the bull back into its pen.

The bull was driven back by him into its pen.

An <u>intransitive verb</u> does not require an object to make sense, nor can it take the passive form:

He ran off at high speed.

She slept until morning.

Some <u>verbs</u> may be <u>transitive</u> or <u>intransitive</u> according to how they are used in a sentence:

I wish I could fly.

I am going out to fly my kite.

5. Clear Essentials:
The one-page guide

—

For those who, like us, love to see the world at a glance, here are our ten essentials of Clear English.

1. Plan what you are going to say or write.

2. Remember who you are writing for.

3. Think clearly to write clearly.

4. Make your points with verve, style and force.

5. Write a draft. Then another. Then another.

6. Then rewrite until you have the best version.

7. Cut useless words and ideas.

8. Check your work.

9. When you have said enough, stop.

10. Never be anyone but yourself.

Thanks to: Janet Beard of Keyword Office Support, Barnaby Harsent, Jim Leaver, Jonathan Lloyd, Mary Loudon, Jo Matches, Kathy Rooney, Kate St George, the staff and directors of Bloomsbury Plc and Oxford Writing Ltd.

Index

___